Simple Social Media

Amp-Up the Voice of Your Business

Russell Mickler

Disclaimer

No patent liability is assumed with respect to the use of the information contained herein. Although every precaution has been taken in the preparation of this book, the publisher and author assume no responsibility for errors or omissions. Nor is any liability assumed for damages resulting from the use of information contained herein. Every effort has been made to make this book as complete and as accurate as possible, but no warranty or fitness is implied. The information is provided on an "as is" basis.

Publisher

Russell Mickler
Mickler & Associates, Inc.
13504 NE 84th Street, STE 103-150
Vancouver, Washington 98682
www.micklerandassociates.com
Voice: 360.216.1784
Fax: 360.397.0468

Errors and Omissions

To report errors and omissions, please send a note to errata@micklerandassociates.com.

Cover Design
Chris Martin of Chris Martin Studios
www.chrismartinstudios.com

Illustrations

Russell Mickler

Trademarks

Bulk Sales

Mickler & Associates, Inc. offers discounts on this book when ordered in quantity for bulk purchases or special sales. For more information, please contact the publisher at booksales@micklerandassociates.com.

Contents

Okay, Now You're Ready to Run!

About the Author

Russell Mickler, Principal Consultant of Mickler & Associates, Inc., has over 16 years of professional experience leading and managing IT organizations. As a technology consultant, Mickler assists small to mid-range businesses with crafting and executing technology strategy. In addition to earning his Master's Degree in technology from the University of Oregon, Mickler is a Computer Information Systems Security Professional (CISSP) and a Microsoft Certified Systems Engineer (MCSE). Mickler teaches graduate and undergraduate technology courses for many universities across the country. Mickler is the co-author of several books concerning Information Technology and Information Security. Mickler is also a public speaker on matters concerning social media and technology, and creates all types of media at micklerandassociates.com and his blog, reinventwork.com. Russell Mickler and Mickler & Associates, Inc. can be found on Facebook, on Twitter at @micklerr, and emailed directly at rmickler@micklerandassociates.com. Simple Social Media is the author's first self-published effort.

Acknowledgements

Thanks to everyone who has supported me over the years, for having faith in what I can accomplish, and for tolerating my sense of humor. No, really: I appreciate it. Thanks.

Reader Feedback and Suggestions

It's my hope that you find this book useful and practical, and as my reader, you're the most important critic in the world. If you have comments or suggestions regarding this book, please feel free to send your ideas my way via email or Facebook. I'd love to receive your feedback.

Reader Services and Materials

Many materials, presentations, videos, and downloadable forms mentioned within this book can be found on the author's website, http://www.micklerandassociates.com/simple-social-media.

Introduction

You're likely the owner of a small business and want to learn how social media can help promote it. At this point, social media might look way too technical and time-consuming with little obvious return, and you're probably wondering where to start. There are so many software tools - Facebook, Twitter, Foursquare, MySpace, Buzz, Plurk, Flickr - and you're wrestling with how to use them. And I'd bet you're more distracted by the tools than the strategy and that's got you frustrated. You're too wrapped up in the *how* than the *why*.

Perfect!

And that's why I wrote this book. I wrote it for you! This book addresses the *why* behind social media. *Why* is it important? *Why* should my business use it? *Why* are others flocking to it? My intention in writing the book is to help clarify the strategic use of social media for the small to mid-range business or what I'd refer to as businesses with up to fifty employees. It's designed to help you understand the *why* and *manage* a social media campaign from start to execution and conclusion.

Luckily for both of us, reading this book is going to be a lot easier than you think. This book isn't overtly technical and there's nothing in here that you probably don't already intuitively know. Social media isn't new to small business; business owners like yourself have been using direct mail marketing, newsletters, presentations, and face-to-face networking to talk about their products and services for a long time, and chances are you're fairly adept at it.

What is new about social media concerns cost and reach. With social media, small business owners have access to thousands upon thousands of people instantly and at practically no cost. Brands can be created, supported, and destroyed virtually overnight from honest – perhaps *too* honest – consumer opinion. Digital relationships, dialog, and feedback can be built between consumers, clients, and suppliers, allowing the small business to get closer to their market than ever before. Social media commands a top-of-mind awareness that traditional media (television, radio, and print) would find difficult to rival.

Now *that* is new!

Meanwhile, the power of word-of-mouth marketing shouldn't be any surprise to you, either. Small business owners have always depended on customer testimonials to promote their businesses in the community. What's different now is that the community is *global* and word-of-mouth can spread at the speed of light. Customer experiences – good and bad - can be instantly shared with hundreds of people with the click of a button.

This book tries to capitalize on your existing skills as a business owner and manager, and apply them to managing a social media campaign. Not to say that we'll skip over the technical aspects of these issues but the *how* behind the technology implementation isn't as important as the *why*. You can always hire the *how* if you're unfamiliar with the tech. However, you can't understand how social media fits into your business model until you get the *why*.

So here's what we're going to be talking about:

- Social Media as a digital printing press and as a transforming technology

- Social Media as a promotion tool, sales channel, and branding mechanism

- Social Media as a means to reach out and listen to your customers

- Social Media as a means to create and maintain a community around your brand

- Social Media as a managed, disciplined approach to reach measurable business objectives

This book complements and consolidates the courses that I prepared for Clark Community College of Vancouver, Washington in 2009 and 2010, and since then, I've tailored this material to seminars, presentations, and corporate training programs. I designed those Clark courses for the average business person so that the content could be immediately applied and reap some benefit for their company in straight-forward, no-nonsense, no-techno-babble way, and that's precisely what I hope you'll find here.

I've written this book to be an exercise in practical advice that anybody who runs a business or non-profit could use immediately – overnight – without too much of a technical background. I assume that you're spending a majority of your time providing the products and services that make your customers happy, and less time banging your noggin against a computer screen for entertainment. Crazy. I also assume that you don't have a great deal of patience for technical jargon that you can't and won't use. Astounding. And I'd also assume you're good at delegation – that you're accustomed to delegating technical aspects of projects like these to talent and then monitoring their progress. Wow.

The content within the book is prepared in bursts: five topical sections that are easily-digestible. It is actually meant to be read cover to cover because concepts explored in one section are then readily applied in subsequent sections. Fear not, though: the book doesn't require you to take notes and there will be no quiz at the end. Instead, the book is meant as a resource for the everyman so that they can get up and running with social media without having to hire expensive consultants, technical experts, or an advertising firm. It's a DIY (Do-It-Yourself) kit to help you manage your own social media strategy and an educational tool to help you have meaningful conversations with your expert resources.

- **Part One** really addresses the nature of social media as a grassroots evolution in digital publishing and as a destabilizing force towards traditional institutions. In order to really understand the way social media is impacting businesses, there has to be a considered look at what social media does to conventional sources of *power*. Social media, in fact, transfers power from traditional institutions (governments, publishers, large media conglomerates, and businesses) to the individual, and social media leverages that power to provide a diversity of opinion that may differ from messages offered by official spokespeople or a slick advertising campaign. As the decentralization of power is what the small business is attempting to tap in to by engaging social media in the first place, it's only fitting that we'd take a good look at its implications before getting started.

- **Part Two** attempts to explain the driving forces behind social media. I've counted nine of them: Groundswell, Community, Trust, Cults of Personality, Mobility, Interconnectedness and Participation, the Long Tail, Free, and

Abundance versus Scarcity. Each driver explains the *why* behind social media – *why* businesses are so interested in it, *why* our customers are flocking to it, *why* social media is transforming the consumer expectations. These are concepts used throughout the social media landscape and their exploration will provide you with a baseline understanding of the tactics and strategies explored in the book.

- **Part Three** is an investigation into the various kinds of technologies employed by social media to achieve our objectives as a small business. I talk at length about the use of your website – your Destination on the web – as a central repository for curated content. I also look at the problem of Search and blogging, and how search engines use content found on your Destination to relate ideas, words, and phrases to your brand. From there, we leap into social networks and microblogging as means to generate community, broadcast updates of our content, pull our audience back to our Destination, and as a means to elicit useful feedback from our customers. And finally, I touch on how social bookmarking, feeds, and tagging facilitates getting our content in front of a potential audience. Again, staying above the technical details that would normally accompany such a conversation, I talk wholly about strategy here, and why these broad-spectrum of tools would be useful to executing a social media campaign.

- **Part Four** invokes the spirit of Peter Drucker to examine the discipline of management through measurements or metrics. Too often, social media initiatives will fail because they lack a material outcome, and by *material* I'm referring to make money, or, somehow contribute to making money. The effectiveness of a social media campaign depends entirely upon the reasonable outcomes we hope to achieve, those whom we'd hold accountable to execute, and to the demonstrative benefit of the organization. If we cannot prove tangible benefit to social media then what would compel anyone to engage it? This section attempts to flatten the argument of "everybody else is doing it" into something more meaningful to your time.

- **Part Five** concludes the book with a discussion on planning and implementation. Grounded with a solid set of theory, now it's time to apply these problems to your business. Combined with tools available from my own website, my reader should be able to take these ideas and apply them strategically in a planned and organized manner. Planning is tantamount to success with social media for it's through the repetitive development and execution of social media campaigns that we demonstrate incremental value to the organization, and our successes may become political instruments to justify continued efforts.

And like many authors, I've also provided an accumulation of tips, illustrations, and commentary throughout the work that may provide additional insight into the subject matter. At the end of each part of the book, I'll pose follow-up questions related to the subject matter that I'll often ask my clients to drill deeper into their organizations' culture. And I'll often refer to content available from my own blog that could be useful in exploring concepts further – just look for the conspicuous B-icon. Links to each of these resources can be found conveniently at http://www.micklerandassociates.com/simple-social-media.

What this book won't do is teach you how to use Facebook, Twitter, or Linked-in, nor will it instruct you on the mystic black arts of influencing search engines. Again, my presumption is you know how to get your hands on such talent or assistance. This isn't a tutorial, a training manual, or a cheap bag of tricks to try with your website. It won't make you money overnight and it's not going to guarantee you 1,000 followers on Twitter by next Tuesday. Rather, what this book will do is explain how you'd practically and strategically use social media to meet your business goals - simply. It's designed as a strategy guide for social media that any small business owner could yank off the shelf and apply tomorrow.

And please *friend*-me on Facebook (www.facebook.com/russell.mickler) to join my community of like-minded professionals looking to leverage social media for the small business.

WORLD.   BOOK.   WEB.   COMMUNITY.

So let's get started.

Part One
What You Will Learn

- How social media is a grassroots evolution of media

- Why social media is democratizing traditional power and diminishing institutional power

- How governments and media are transforming to the new power dynamic

- How the decentralization of power offers competitive advantages for small business

- How business strategy is evolving to take advantage of social media

Why?

When I talk to a small business owner about social media that's usually the first question I get. And it's not that this person is resistant to change, hates technology, lives under a rock, or doesn't understand the importance of the Internet; they're smart, rational people who've ran successful businesses for years. It's just, well, "why?"

"There's no ROI," would be their follow-up comment and then followed by (and this one's a classic): "I don't care what somebody ate for lunch."

Comments like these are dismissive, of course, because very few people want to listen to a consultant convince them they need something and I'm supposed to shut-up. Luckily I'm terrible at that and - after ten minutes of conversation - that same small business owner will look me dead in the eye and ask me:

"Nobody's ever explained it like that - how do we get started?"

Why a Social Networking Strategy is Important

So it turns out that everybody they ever met explained social media from the perspective of its tools rather than a business strategy. This is what Twitter is; here's what Facebook does; this how you access YouTube; here's the way it looks on your phone and – so-help-me – maybe sixty-percent of the time, their tutor was a teenager.

Further, if they adventurously began using some of these tools they most likely saw a lot of lost souls trying to find their voice without a practical education, or, helplessly witnessed their own employees wasting tons of company time playing Farmville. Inundated by the complexities of the tech and negatively-impressed by others using the media, they were never offered a compelling "why" to negate their initial impressions that social media is, yes, a giant, fruitless time-suck.

Tools are just tools. Twitter is no more going to help a small business owner increase sales volume than a hammer is going to help a carpenter build a house. Getting a couple of "likes" on Facebook doesn't mean much of anything. I found the small business owner often needed a practical understanding of how the tools could be used to achieve some end objective. In addition, what they lacked was an understanding of the forces driving social media, and practical, no-nonsense strategies for leveraging those forces for their business. They needed a strategic plan, sure, but they also needed somebody to paint the bigger picture to answer "why". Why should they be paying attention to social media at all? Why should they care?

Nobody had ever helped them make that connection before. And that's where we're going to start.

The Digital Printing Press

Throughout all of modern history, mass media and distribution has always been controlled by a few. Governments, aristocrats, capitalists, companies - institutions of many kinds have solely controlled the means of reproducing and distributing ideas. If you wanted to write a book, air a video, perform a play, or record a song, you had to convince these institutions to take a risk, finance its production, and reproduce the content. And because the means of reaching vast audiences was so expensive, they filtered all but the most profitable projects from distribution in order to guarantee a healthy return for their financial risk.

Media institutions long cultivated a relationship between distribution and advertising. Content delivered across television, radio, and print were expensive channels, and advertising revenue directly influenced the development, production, and circulation of programming. What was produced is what would sell. Only the top authors, the top movies, the top musicians, and the content of top corporations were presented to the mindshare of the consuming public. Everything else was filtered because it was deemed either unworthy or unprofitable.

If you're paying attention, you might find it curious that I continue to talk about mass media in the past-tense? You see, around the year 2000, technologies on the Internet evolved to a point where the everyday Joe could become their own publisher of digital content and distribute it for free across the Internet. And as the technologies evolved, even the most unskilled could contribute audio, video, software, graphics, pictures, or written narrative, and the cost to produce, store, and send these products to everybody in the world was practically nil. Everyone owned their own digital printing press in the form of personal computers. Social media was born. But where does that leave us today?

The Slow, Agonizing Death of Traditional Media

Things aren't looking too hot right now if you're working in traditional media. The business model is broken and advertisers are abandoning ship. Newspaper advertising revenue in the United States has declined 33.4% percent since 2008 to $28.4 billion industry-wide; television in the US is has 22.4% declines in expected annual revenue; magazine publishers are posting anywhere from 18%-26% annual declines in advertising revenue; and in radio, US advertising is expected to fall a full 45.5% from 2008 levels. Subscriptions are falling, readership is dwindling – dying, really - and talent is departing due to rapid changes in the way people consume media.

Yikes!

Technology changed the business model of media and consumer expectation from one of scarcity to abundance faster than traditional media could change its business model.

- Instead of a few channels, consumers have access to hundreds of channels.

- Instead of a few programs, consumers have access to thousands of programs.

- Instead of watching commercials, consumers can conveniently edit them out of the video stream.

- Instead of having finite choice in scheduling, consumers can schedule their media consumption around their own schedule.

- Instead of radio, television, or print, consumers are devouring podcasts, streaming video, and blogs.

- Instead of televisions, radios, or paper, consumers are digesting their content across phones, tablets, and PC's.

Abundance trumps scarcity and consumers really dig *infinite*. The problem is that *infinite* is pretty darn expensive and abundant consumer choice means a much smaller audience to receive institutional advertising, which – in turn - blows away their revenue model.

Woops. There goes that modern mass media stuff we were discussing earlier and it's regrettably a slow, agonizing death for these companies.

Tastes and preferences have changed, technologies and delivery mechanisms have changed, and the producers have changed – from big, corporate institutions to anyone with a digital printing press – demanding a complete re-think of that sector to survive. Right now, traditional media is undergoing a dramatic, competitive evolution rife with acquisitions, cost-cutting, and re-imagining what physical media can be, and how it can compete against an abundance of bits.

An Abundance of Bits

You might be familiar with Moore's Law. It's a technology industry principle that's held true for half a century that basically says the power of computing doubles every eighteen months whereas its cost drops by half. Some even suggest that time-frame has been cut in half to just nine months. What it suggests is that technology gets faster and cheaper every day. Moore's Law has proven very consistent and is unlikely to change in the near future.

There's a corresponding set of laws that concern hard disk space and bandwidth that suggest the same thing: over time, the capacity to store and transmit bits grows exponentially while the price of the technology becomes less expensive.

Inexpensive, fast technology has allowed businesses to replace physical paper with electronic data; labor with automation and software; warehouses with hard drives; and trucks with fiber optics. Instead of physical stores with thousands of books and movies, we can access online catalogs of millions of titles instantaneously, and to expand that catalog by a million more titles would cost the distributor next to nothing. Business automation has allowed organizations to achieve massive economies of scale where the highest productivity can be achieved with the lowest possible investment in labor. Capitalism - the profit motive - has encouraged mass investment in bits.

We live in a world that's just abundant with bits. Most of us have devices that process bits on our person at all times. Business, entertainment, news, information, video, music, books – all of media – are just bits. Bits provide for an infinite array of consumer choice and enables the growth of social media.

So What is Social Media?

The digital printing press combined with an abundance of bits removes the power once held by institutions, aristocrats, capitalists, corporations, governments, and religions and transfers that power to the individual. It is the elimination of institutional censorship – for reasons that were economic, political, sociological, ideological, or otherwise – that represents the real reason why social media is so significant and so important.

That has never happened before in the scope of human history. And we are experiencing the first ten years of such a phenomenal change in cultural power first-hand, right now.

Wow. As Marty McFly once said, "Heavy".

All of the factors of production have been reduced to bits, and media of all types can now be generated by anybody, reproduced by anybody, distributed by anybody, and consumed by anybody anywhere at zero marginal cost. In the last decade, the tools that enable the production and transportation of digital content vastly matured, and the uncensored, grass-roots ideas that were created by individuals using free electronic tools is the essence of social media.

Social media:

- is intellectual property (text, video, audio, software) developed by ordinary people and not by mass media institutions, governments, large organizations, professional journalists, or even trained artists;

- is highly individualized, niched, uncensored, and subjective;

- is entrepreneurial;

- supports broad democratic principles like free speech and freedom of the press;

- thrives off consumer trust, word-of-mouth, and personal referrals;

- is free, reusable, repeatable, and easily distributed as it's electronic and pliable.

- is often influenced by cults of personality who win the trust of consumers.

- is collaborative and attracts a community of participants and spectators.

Already a decade has gone by and it's hard to entirely ascertain the magnitude of transformation social media will have on institutional power, but the demise of traditional forms of mass media (radio, television, and print) over the distribution of *ideas* is clearly at hand. We are living in an amazing age – an era where everyone on the planet has the ability express themselves and share ideas effortlessly to an audience of millions. And I think, if you're a small business owner, you should be thinking: what is your small business, your brand, your product ... going to say in that vast conversation? What will your *ideas* be?

Social Media ... By the Numbers

 Facebook Facts

Now, very briefly, I'm going to bombard you with a great number of statistics that will be overwhelming and yet justify my position that social media is relevant and important – it's a technique that they teach us in consulting school to hypnotize our prey (ahem, I mean, "clients") and stun them into submission. I'll only do this once in the whole darn book, I promise. Here it goes:

In a survey conducted by the Society for New Communications Research, a growing number of consumers use social media in the following ways[1]:

- 59-percent of respondents use social media to "vent" about a customer experiences

- 72-percent of respondents research companies' customer experiences

- 84-percent of respondents consider the quality of customer experiences at least sometimes in their decision to do business with a company

- 74-percent choose companies/brands based on others' experiences shared online

- 81-percent believe that blogs, online rating systems and discussion forums can give consumers a greater voice

- Less than 33-percent believe that businesses take customers' opinions seriously

Further, as reported in an October 2010, Inc. Magazine article[2]:

- 70-percent of consumers are more likely to do buy from a local business if it has information about its products and services available on a social media website;

- 81-percent of consumers using social media say it's important for businesses to respond to questions and complaints;

- 78-percent of consumers using social media said reviews and ratings offered by social media sites on local businesses are important when deciding what to buy;

- 78-percent of consumers using social media want special offers, promotions, information, and news from companies with a presence on social media sites;

- 74-percent want posts about the company itself whereas more than two-thirds of those surveyed wanted to see internal photos, like, of the company picnic;

- Social networking consumers are 67-percent more likely to buy something than a general internet user, and one-in-six searchers is frustrated with the lack of reliable information about small businesses on the web (information is contradictory, confusing, or disorganized); one-third of searchers give up on a local business because they can't find what they're looking for;

- 70-percent of consumers go online first for local business information, whereas 23 percent still turn to the Yellowpages.

Some social media statistics also seem to suggest having Facebook fans is advantageous. Among the top reasons consumers had for "liking" a company's Facebook page[3]:

- 49-percent were previous customers and wanted to identify as such;

- 42-percent wanted to show their support for the brand, product, or service;

- 40-percent of consumers wanted access to discounts and promotions offered across that channel;

- 34-percent just found it fun and entertaining!

Wow, when's the last time you thought of your brand as "fun and entertaining?"

Meanwhile, as you're thinking about that, here are some additional ideas from Lauren Bianchi's ViralBlog. A study of over 1,500 consumers on Facebook and Twitter concluded[4]:

- Facebook users that "Friended" or LIKED a product/business page were 51-percent more likely to buy; that number was 67-percent from Twitter users;

- Similarly, 60-percent of Facebook users in the survey that "Friended" or LIKED a product/business page were more likely to recommend others to product/brand; 79-percent for Twitter users.

And yet more juicy factors that should command at least some of your attention. Given all of these ideas that I've mentioned, in July 2010, Neilsen found that[5]:

- Spending time on social networks is the biggest thing people do on the Internet;

- Americans spend 1/3 of their online time communicating across the web with social media;

- 48-percent of customers use blogs and other forms of social networking to talk about their experiences with brands;

- Over 100 million people are on Twitter, and more than 600 million on Facebook;

- More than fifty percent of Facebook's user base logs in each day (some 300 million people – just a bit shy of the entire population of the United States).

And finally, let's wrap up with some testimonial-based perceptions from consumers about brands uninvolved with social networking[6]:

- "It's EXPECTED that a company have some digital face – whether it's on FB or Twitter, I don't know – but they need a strong electronic presence or you doubt their relevance in today's marketplace." (Female 50-54)

- "Either they are not interested in the demographic that frequents Facebook and Twitter or they are unaware of the opportunity to get more exposure in a more interactive method." (Male 35-39)

- "It shows they are not really with it or in tune with the new ways to communicate with customers." (Female 18-24)

- "If they're not on Facebook or Twitter, then they aren't in touch with the "electronic" people." (Female 55-59)

When looking at numbers, trends, demographics, and comments like these, or at the way that consumers are using social media to connect to local companies, or at consumer's perception of businesses that don't use social media – the value of social media should be patently clear.

It'd be a mistake to simply accept these statistics at face-value and presume that all of your customers are waiting for you on social media outlets, and that all of your customers use social media, and that social media should displace your current advertising strategy. That isn't necessarily the case. Social media may not even be a great fit for your brand, products, or customer base. However, the bounty of evidence should at least compel some critical thought: there are a lot of expectations from consumers driving social media adoption. Putting your head in the sand to wait for the fad to pass your company by may be a significant mistake or missed opportunity. Although I'd be the last to encourage you to jump off of the bridge with everybody else, with such incredible feedback on consumer preferences and opinion, further investigation into social media should at least appear prudent.

So long as I've convinced you that social media is worth study, I might be able to present you with a world of possibilities and deliver some value out of this book for you. An even though social media may look scary and nearly impossible to define right now, I'm going to take a few minutes now to explain why social media is nothing new and that you already know how to do it.

The Small Business

Small business is the backbone of American prosperity. Small businesses offer independence, innovation, and entrepreneurship that typifies American economic strength.

Common problems encountered when launching a small business are widely understood. You need a good plan, the right people, a little seed money, a great pitch, and a little twist of luck to convince investors to loan startup capital.

Yet the hardest part about starting a business isn't these things. Rather it's convincing consumers to stop by your store, to encourage them to ask questions, to showcase your products, and to convince a customer to buy. The first decision to buy may be one of expediency, convenience, or or necessity – you're just around at the right time and at the right place to be awarded the sale. Over time, though, the second, third, and fourth decision to buy is one based entirely on *trust*. Consumers will only return to spend more of their money on your products and service if you've convinced them that you're worthy of their trust. Cultivating consumer trust is the single most important activity performed by a business because – over time – we, as consumers, don't buy always things from producers out of necessity but out of loyalty. The hardest part about starting a business is getting a consumer to trust you and to remain loyal to you, your brand, and your company.

Successful small business entrepreneurs figured out how to earn consumer trust by doing three things very well:

- They let their customers know what they're about: their values, principles, niche, products, and services;

- They keep a consistent standard of quality when providing their products and services;

- They establish relationships with their customers.

What's Your Core Competency?

In consultant-jive we call these activities the *core competencies* of a business.
Every business concern has to do these things well – consistently - in order to be
profitable and to grow. If it can't, then the company won't be able to develop in its
niche, continuously impress its customers, grow trust and encourage their referral
to others, or bring more meaning to their customer's lives beyond the single
financial transaction. Relative obscurity, chronic ineptitude that will erode
profitability and confidence, and an underdeveloped word-of-mouth marketing
message, will eventually kill the business.

CORE COMPETENCIES.

Getting Measurable Results from IT Spending

With the fall of institutional power and traditional mass media, social media can be
leveraged by a business to continuously exercise its core competencies. Just as
social media is used to create and sustain interpersonal relationships among
people, social media represents a real opportunity for the small business to build
relationships with their customers and to foster a sense of community around a
shared sense of values, to illustrate their passion and commitment to what they do,
and to learn from their customers to correct their mistakes.

Constant reinforcement of a business' core competencies bestows more
opportunity to win-over the trust of consumers. Simply, people do business in the
long-term with who they trust. Consumers buy brands that they've come to trust
and love, around which they've cultivated years of loyalty, and they'll only
recommend trusted brands, products, services, and companies to others. Social
media allows a company to inexpensively talk about what differentiates them from
the competition; it allows a company to listen and respond directly to consumer

feedback and opinion; it gives a company means of creating more trust with consumers.

The Age of Trust

We in the pompous practice of punditry and prognostication have officially declared our times the Age of Trust, in fact, as it would appear human relationships are fast becoming the foundation for loyalty, commerce, and authority. Who you deem trustworthy – in terms of friends, celebrities, institutions, brands, or products - will entirely shape your opinions and behaviors. How you receive news, information, and opinion is entirely shaped by trust; how well you accept recommendations and referrals from others about local businesses is shaped by your trust around others; what you're willing to buy, do, visit, or engage in, is married to the trust you have in that institution or the consistency of that experience; who we trust is even reduced to as score cards on social networks, and an activity in our modern times – a verb – like "friending". And as social media both enhances and builds trust between people, brands, and products, it's considered the principal vehicle driving the Age of Trust into even deeper territory.

 So ... Do You Trust Me?

Social media creates, fosters, enhances, and encourages trust. Insasmuch, social media allows small businesses to get closer to their target consumer more than any other time in modern history and at practically zero-cost. Because the importance placed on being "local", "small", "neighborly" are so relevant in today's marketplace, Social media can be a powerful mechanism that small businesses can use to thrive within an economy hobbled by recession, thrift, and consumer anxiety. Social networks are quickly becoming the tools consumers use to refer their friends, family, and colleagues to trusted businesses and services.

Sharing

Social Media isn't developed under the same principles that have guided mass media. It is biased, subjective, uncensored, and sometimes downright crude; equally so, social media is also thoughtful, real, sincere, and reflects the intensity of its authors; it may be factually inaccurate, slanderous, and appalling; it may appear professional, well thought out, tirelessly edited, and profound. Social Media is all of these things.

But most of all, social media is *shared*. Creator/owners of social media reflect on the stuff created by others and share it with others within their extended network. In a world of interconnectedness, we are millions of experts and authorities contributing to a larger dialog of things meaningful to each one of us, around which self-interested communities are built. Sharing what we find online is a matter of participation and engagement, an activity that helps continue a long-standing narrative that we're all immersed in: our daily lives.

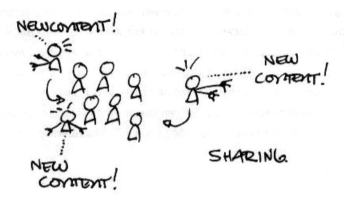

Sharing is something American children are taught to do at a very early age. Sharing is a demonstration of yielding power; of sacrifice; of community; of valuing a benefit larger than just yourself. Sharing is "good" behavior insofar that we've assigned a moral meaning to it in our culture. Sharing allows us to "get along" and collaborate in an environment of shared risk. Sharing is the foundation idea behind social networks. Whether or not I'm sharing my ideas, thoughts, and experiences; pictures, activities, or hobbies; a positive or poor experience that I had with a business, product, or brand; a new activity that I'd like everyone to try for themselves; or new social media that I happened to come across online.

Yet despite our up-bringing as American children, as adults, sharing has an implied stigma: we can share *too* much. So much that the information or ideas we might share could be considered extraneous or irrelevant or insulting – it may even diminish our standing, or, foster unconfirmed opinion, hurt others, may make us appear conceded or self-indulgent or arrogant, or may make us less-competitive.

Whereas we were taught the ropes of sharing as children, by our adult years, we will have learned the consequences of sharing too much and will instead *horde:* as a cultural survival mechanism, we may share very little as not to expose our position, or, share little as to hope others don't think less of us.

Unless you're under the age of twenty, I'd be willing to venture that – within you – there's an inner struggle between these two forces when you're using social media. How much do I share? How much would be reasonable and appropriate? How little should I share? What should I say?

This sensation will be normal for anybody who is not relatively young - I mention the age of twenty because anyone younger than that has been sharing nearly all aspects of their life in near-real-time since the dawn of their cognitive ability; i.e., the average teenager texts over 3,370 messages per month. Sharing nearly every thought, idea, opinion, and notion nearly instantly isn't foreign to this age group, and sharing is promoted and encouraged in their sub-culture much more so than in my generation, or my parents, or my grand-parents generation. This isn't 'bad' or 'wrong' and it'll do you well to suspend such moral judgments on their behavior – it simply *is* - and overcoming the impulse to share *less* may be one of the most challenging aspects of using social media for you. Yet sharing is the underpinning of your success; should you embrace it, you will become accustomed to sharing more by the time this process is said and done with. Successful businesses in the Age of Trust share more and are very transparent in their dealings with customers. Just remember: sharing isn't *bad* and t may take you a while to master it again. Be patient with yourself.

And sharing is best facilitated by networks of relationships that tie people together.

What are Social Networks?

Networks consist of ties and nodes. In technology, a great example of a network is a computer connected to a network that allows it to participate on the Internet. The Internet is a vast network of communication ties and node computers.

Socially, people are nodes bound by ties of human relationships. Friends, colleagues, work associates, students and instructors, or family – webs of connections that define our role in our lives, our experiences, and our expertise –

and social networks aren't anything new; complex interrelationships between human beings have always existed. What's different today is that technology automates, facilitates, and extends those relationships. Without the aid of technology, we'd reach diminishing levels of return – we couldn't possibly maintain so many relationships in the amount of time that's available to us. Without the devices, software, and computers we use day in and day out, humans would gravitate to relating in much smaller circles constrained by time, distance, and capacity. And this is an important point: social networks don't necessarily displace the human experience but instead help manage, automate, and extend the complexity of human relationships.

- Facebook doesn't displace or replace interacting with your kids; it augments that interaction by sharing in their personal experience.

- Twitter doesn't displace or replace the need for a phone call; it can be used to share meaningful information without the phone call.

- Neither Facebook nor Twitter displace or replace the importance of interpersonal relationships with your customers, your friends, family, or high school pals; they can be used to help support those relationships, share in a common experience, and build trust.

- Foursquare doesn't displace or replace the experience of being somewhere; it brings others with you, virtually, to share your experience.

- Skype doesn't displace or replace the value of a face-to-face meeting; it makes it easier to meet face-to-face when doing so is just impractical or impossible.

Social networks leverage Internet technology to offer a greater economy-of-scale in managing our relationships. They don't displace or replace but augment. With less time and effort, social networking allows us to interrelate with many others and *share* at the speed of light all across the world, sharing ideas, inner-most thoughts, pictures and video, exciting or dry experiences – even, yes, what we may have had for lunch. Mobile devices allow us to remain interconnected almost all of the time and everywhere we are.

Business Strategy, Social Media, and Social Networking

Why a Social Networking Strategy is Important

Now, at first glance, the importance of the ability to share what I had for lunch with two-hundred friends may seem ridiculous. And many would probably argue that the "meaningfulness" of having hundreds of electronic "friends" is a pleasant euphemism – we can't possibly have hundreds of meaningful relationships; all of those ties are, at best, vague names in a huge Rolodex. So the word 'friend' and 'share' is probably an overstatement of our emotional commitment to our online acquaintances. You are so right!

Still, what's important to business here is how ideas, opinions, perceptions, and experiences are proliferated across ties from one node to the next in an almost infectious, viral pattern.

And therein lies the promise for business. If a brand can positively influence just one highly-connected individual in a large social network of thousands of people, then they're able to leverage the trust all of those people have in that one party to recommend their product or service.

Kathy Condon
I need to gravel/apologize to a radio host on the East Coast--we got the time difference mixed up--missed the call. What could I send him from the NW that would be a nice gesture?
January 12 at 9:44am · Like · Comment

Russell Mickler Liquid Gratitude ... http://www.liquidgratitude
.com/ - local business, good unique NW packages; look for Mickey
Lane, owner. Tell her I sent ya (grin).
January 12 at 9:49am · Like

Going yet another step further, that brand may be able to translate their influence within these networks into action. Maybe it's to encourage a consumer to buy something; to subscribe to a newsletter; to visit a website; to read an article or a white paper; to enlist, volunteer, or donate; to engage in a dialog; to watch a video; to share a picture or an experience. The social network becomes a way to leverage trust and encourage an action.

Thereafter, the desired results are quite favorable. Brand exposure will go up; its message will proliferate to the desktop and cell phones of thousands; leads will increase; sales will rise; consumer involvement and participation will increase; more constructive feedback will be captured and responded to; goodwill towards a brand will build. Influencing even a tiny fraction of a social network is a winning strategy for your business.

On the flip-side, if a brand influences a high-connected individual in a social network of thousands through a poor experience then the consequences could be dire. Raw, uncensored consumer opinion could re-define a national brand that took decades to hone in just hours. Consumer attitudes towards products, services, motivations, and interests could implode; sales could diminish, interest could fade, negativism towards the company could dominate the dialog, and your brand could be irreparably harmed. That's a losing social media strategy for your business.

Overnight, social media has become the *voice of your business*. That presents an opportunity to exercise your core competencies and engage the consumer on new and exciting levels, and that calls for taking control of social media to manage it, direct it, and shape it. There's an incredible number of things that social media can help a business strategically accomplish:

- Social Media can help shape our brand and company's image in the digital age;

- Social Media can help a company get closer to its customers, engage them, solicit their feedback, and learn how to meet their needs;

- Social Media can help us talk to customers on a very personal level to gain their trust and attention, and to be allowed in their inner circle of acquaintances and friends;

- Social Media allows companies to promote their ideas, products, values, and services to an attentive "always-on" niche marketplace at zero marginal cost (for free!)

- Social Media encourages transparency and can personalize, build, and reinforce a brand, and establish credibility;

- Social Media encourages our audience (our customers) to act.

Now that we've taken some time to explore terms and strategies, the concepts behind social media and social networks may sound a bit more concrete and perhaps a bit more compelling. I'd also be willing to bet social media sounds a bit more important to you. But to manage it, you need to understand where social media is coming from and where it's going – its driving forces. That's what we'll explore next.

Follow-up Questions

1. Does your senior management team clearly know what social media and social networks are, and their importance in earning the trust of consumers?

2. Is there a marketing awareness taking place in your company that social media is becoming increasingly important, or, are there heads in the sand?

3. How is your current social media strategy creating trust, leveraging social networks, and encouraging action? Are those activities being measured?

4. Is there a single role responsible and accountable for social media within your organization?

5. How is your social media strategy exercising your core competencies?

6. Does your current social media strategy listen to your customers? Social media should listen and respond to consumers; it should accept and act upon constructive feedback. How are you listening? How are you responding?

7. How are your competitors leveraging social media to establish a rapport with their customers? How are they promoting their products and reinforcing their brand online?

8. What do your customers want? How do they want to relate to your business online?

9. How is Abundance playing in your competitive strategy? What products, services, and value can your business leverage as bits?

10. How well does your company Share?

References

1. No Author. No Date. "Social Network Watch: Customer Care Reputation Studied Online Before Making Purchases." Found on the Internet on December 1, 2010: URL: http://www.socialnetworkingwatch.com/2008/05/customer-care-r.html.

2. Rubin, Courtney. October 18, 2010. "Is the Online Information About Your Business Correct?" Inc. Magazine. Found on the Internet on December 1, 2010. URL: http://www.inc.com/news/articles/2010/10/consumers-more-likely-to-use-businesses-active-on-social-media.html

3. Dingra, Rajiv. March 22, 2010. "Social Media 'Does' Influence Buying Decisions." SocialTrakr.com. Found on the Internet on December 1, 2010. URL: http://www.socialtrakr.com/2010/03/22/social-media-does-influence-buying-decisions/

4. Bianchi, Laurens. March 25, 2010. "Does Social Media Affect Buying Behavior?" ViralBlog. Found on the Internet on December 1, 2010. URL: http://www.viralblog.com/research/social-media-affects-consumer-buying-behavior/

5. Gburzynski, Shannon. October 8, 2010. "3 Reasons Why You Need Social Media for Customer Service." 7 Summits Agency. Found on the Internet on December 1, 2010. URL: http://www.7summitsagency.com/community/7-summits-blog/blog/tags/social_listening

6. Bianchi, Laurens. March 25, 2010. "Does Social Media Affect Buying Behavior?" ViralBlog. Found on the Internet on December 1, 2010. URL: http://www.viralblog.com/research/social-media-affects-consumer-buying-behavior/

**Part Two
What You Will Learn**

- The driving forces behind social media

- An introduction to new economy vocabulary

- How social media is transforming consumer expectations

- Where and how are these forces manifesting?

What's Driving Social Media?

At this time, I'd like to draw your attention to the man behind the curtain. He's a funny-lookin' guy without a lot of makeup. Pay no attention to Facebook; Twitter is a noisy illusion; Foursquare is just a game you play on a mobile phone; Quora is just an online survey. Tools are simply distractions and they're not directly relevant to your success in leveraging social media for your business.

Now, I'd like to encourage you to pay attention to the broader forces that are driving and shaping social media rather than the headlines, hype, personal opinions, tools, and interim manifestations of those trends. I believe that if you can understand those broader forces then you're more likely to be able to manage them - and use them - to your advantage.

Here's a list of the forces we'll talk about that are driving social media:

- Groundswell

- Community

- Trust

- Cults of Personality

- Mobility

- Interconnectedness and Participation

- The Long Tail

- Free

- Abundance versus Scarcity

Certainly I wouldn't claim this list to be absolute and definitive – there are a lot of reasons why social media is gaining traction in popular culture. However, I believe these ideas are the most important to understand if you're a business owner thinking about developing a social media strategy. Beyond the statistics, these are the reasons why social media is important to you.

Groundswell

This concept is reflected in the remarkable book of the same title written by Charlene Li and Josh Bernoff. *Groundswell* reflects upon the impact of the digital printing press and the debasing of institutional power. There are a couple of core principles that describe Groundswell:

1. Companies must listen to what customers are saying to gain better understanding of how they're meeting or missing their expectations.

2. Through the use of social media and social networking tools, companies can begin talking and can spread their message to consumers.

3. Companies can leverage social media and social networking to energize consumer enthusiasm for a brand, and even make the more influential within those networks evangelists for a brand.

4. Through the use of social media and social networking tools, companies can support their customers directly, or, they can help customers support themselves, or, they can help foster a community of support among their customers.

In the Age of Trust, Groundswell principles are driving social media adoption by businesses everywhere. If there's anything you should remember about groundswell is that it's founded on listening to consumers. Even if you aren't saying anything back, if you're listening, you can make incredible changes from the feedback offered by others.

Yet listening isn't always enough. Groundswell's authors suggest as I do that institutions that have long controlled the mass distribution of ideas are quickly eroding; newspapers, television broadcasters, magazines, radio, and even governments must transform to remain relevant in a world of new media. And many are. The shift of power from institutions to individuals demands a more two-way conversation - brands, products, services, and values are the narrative in an on-going dialog of ideas.

Groundswell principles assert that it behooves companies to listen to their consumers and engage them in a dialog rather than ignore them - or at worse - attempt to silence them. They also suggest that companies have a voice within the new media and should exercise their core competencies within it. Groundswell promotes the idea of evangelists to corporations – companies should actively cultivate the enthusiasm of some consumers to help promote brands to wider-reaching social networks. And Groundswell encourages the use of social networks to extend the support capabilities of the company through creating a community of consumers who can help each other.

Groundswell principles are important because they reflect the new reality of a marketplace of ideas and of sharing ideas that isn't likely to go away. I believe embracing groundswell is paramount to your understanding and leveraging social media. Consider the inverse consequences should we attempt to ignore or prevent the use of social media:

1.   Our company shouldn't listen to its customers or take any of their suggestions into consideration.

2.   Our company has nothing useful to say to an audience of millions.

3.   Our company doesn't actually believe in – or feels passionately about – what it does.

4.   Our company finds no value in extending support to our customers or fostering a community to help answer their questions; they're on their own.

5.   Our company does not find what others have to say or contribute valuable.

6.   Our company isn't transparent nor are we open in our business dealings.

7.   Our company extends no value beyond the initial transaction.

8.   There is no reason for anyone to Trust our company and we certainly don't want to make it easier for you to refer others to us.

9.   Our company would like to avoid being seen, discussed, or talked about. We like our cave. Please go away.

10. There's no value in sharing anything with anybody.

I mean, if social media is the voice of your business, is this what your company wants to be saying? Is this really what you want consumers want to hear from your marketing strategy? I'd imagine not.

Community

It's in the human condition to be a part of something much larger than ourselves. The Internet has long offered an inexpensive means of participating in extended

communities who share similar goals, interests, and ambitions. As of late, the
technologies which allow for participation have afforded more natural interaction
online inclusive of pictures, graphics, video, voice, and text. To today's consumer,
the digital community is simply a real-time extension of their onground relationships
and experiences that are shared, recycled, and widely distributed, and in the new
world, sharing is a form of digital currency. The more you share, the more clout you
are able to have with that community.

Social Media Ain't Private

Social networking is an extension of an old idea in computing called *convergence*.
This was a term used back in the 1980's and 1990's that foretold of a time where
computing and telephony would merge: a computer would become a
communications device and both would become indistinguishable from each other.
Indeed, it's hard not to see the effects of convergence all around us; social tools
that instantly – digitally – interconnects all of us are simply an extension of
convergence.

Convergence transformed the endlessly dull microcomputer that was really good at doing repetitive business tasks into something fun. The computer evolved into a device where you could interact with your friends, share ideas, upload content, play games, and even find love. Convergence helped change the cold, calculator-like computer into a warm, interactive social device. It's what brought the masses to computing whereas geeks like me had been using computers for purely functional purposes.

A dictionary will define community as a group having common ownership, interests, goals, or environment; a community is a "fellowship" of like-minded individuals. Communities are gathered around values, goals, and a shared perception of reality or even a shared perception of risk. Communities will shrink and grow, evolve and transform, in a process that would appear more organic than designed or orchestrated. Communities are "sticky". Communities have a life of their own.

What communities aren't are a bunch of people huddled around a corporate logo, or a blog post, or a new picture, hailing it, and waiting for the next post or picture to comes along. Communities aren't created nor defined by tools (Twitter, Facebook, Plurk, etc.) nor the content that's placed there, or for that matter, the digital devices that enable the content to be interacted with. Where digital devices might facilitate and sustain a community they don't necessarily create it or give it purpose. Communities that work will survive and outlive the tool – they share interests, purpose, and passions that are infinitely larger than the tool. Tools by themselves don't create community. Communities share something bigger than the content itself; than the tools that help enable it; something bigger than just having a profile on Facebook or Twitter. Community isn't a natural extension of a tool.

There's a clear distinction here. There's something bigger to community than the tool. Your work in using social media will be to create communities within it that share in like-minded values, intent, and purpose of your brand. Online communities work for enterprises when they're centered around a common purpose and idea. The big trick to creating an online community won't be to simply join a social network; it'll be to think about what values, purposes, and ideas your brands, products, and services represent, and how those ideas should be shared with others in a way it'll stick. It'll be your work to find, create, and sustain communities using the tools offered social media.

Sarah Kessler, a graduate of Northwestern University's Medill School of
Journalism, recently presented a post on Mashable.com on how to create a world-
class online community for businesses[3]:

1. **Identify Business Objectives.** Know your objectives before going in;
    don't pour resources into attempting to create a community unless you're
    clear about what outcomes you're expecting from it.

2. **Emphasize Being Personal.** A personal touch is important in an online
    community's success; simple things like completing profiles, putting in
    actual pictures of people instead of logos, and letting the community know
    that self-identity is important.

3. **Create a Culture of Belonging.** Welcome every new member that joins
    your community. Greet them with a welcome message and connect them
    with others in the community, just like a good host at a dinner party.

4. **Be a Source for Relevant Content.** Become a great source of content for
    a topic or the business that you're in. Show your expertise. Blend your
    perception and opinion with the latest news and information. Finding
    answers are important to customers. Help them with the answers.

5. **Leverage the Wisdom of the Crowd.** Allow the community to answer
    their own questions; encourage participation and engagement not just to
    the facilitator but between other community members.

6. **Highlight Influential Members.** Leaders have a direct impact upon other
    users in the community. Through engaging and highlighting your biggest
    fans, you'll empower them to help shape and grow your community.

7. **Reward Members in Pixels, not Pennies.** Here's a new idea for you:
    digital recognition. How can you use the media to provide nearly costless,
    abundant rewards and incentives?

8. **Establish and Enforce Guidelines.** Create policies and procedures that
    identify what your employees and members of the community can and
    can't do, and how violations to that policy can be handled.

9. **Give Members Privileges.** Non-members should be treated a little differently from members in order to provide incentive for others to join the community. Examples could be access to special content, discounts, coupons, or just access to others in the community.

Fostering community and nurturing relationships between people who've the same shared values will be at the center of your work with social media. You'll also be measuring the impacts of your own celebrity and your own influence within that community. Creating and monitoring that "something else" beyond the tool will factor into a large part of your success. In the final analysis, it'd be valuable to look at community as a process that builds and evolves and transforms over time rather than something that's inherently acquired through an online presence.

Trust

I've already spoken at length about the Age of Trust. Who do you "follow"? Who do you "friend"? What are brands, organizations, politicians, charities, and individuals saying that motivate, compel, or inspire? As a small business owner, how do you get someone to trust you and to do business with you? Don't we all prefer to do business with people we know and trust?

In the Age of Trust, who you know matters, and who you convince to trust you matters even more. Who you know can recommend the best brands, products, and services in a closely-knit word-of-mouth referral network. Who you know can influence opinion, shape ideas, compel to act, and encourage a vote. Some even call Trust more important than Search when it comes to marketing your business.

Think about it: if you're to ask a search engine for the best Thai restaurant in your neighborhood, what are you going to get back? A list organized in some arcane means of relevance that might be close to your general proximity. Further investigation of each element within that list could give you insight on where to go for lunch.

On the other hand, you trust your friends. What if you were to ask your social network where the best Thai restaurant in your neighborhood would be? The results could be more informative and reliable, and my guess is that you'll trust your friend more than Google, and that's the point.

Trust is big. Trust has the potential to dramatically reshape digital marketing and diminish the importance of search engines in favor of social networks. Trust can debase over fifteen years of Internet marketing strategy through SEO (Search Engine Optimization) in a blink of an eye, because we're not relying upon technology to help lead us to a Destination. Instead, our social ties and the recommendations of others can.

Trust is the business plan for Facebook, Twitter, Flickr, and others, and that's why social networking is so important to your business strategy. They're betting their farm on the idea that people trust each other more than Internet search engines, and that more people will use social networks to make decisions. With Trust, it doesn't matter how clever or pretty or expensive your website is. If consumers are bypassing search engines in favor of obtaining information on products and services, and moving into their social networks to help make that decision, it'd seem very critical that you were somehow represented in that process.

Cults of Personality

 Your Own Celebrity

In social networking, you are the star! Constant interconnectedness gives us an inspired glimpse into who we are as people and not just as businesses or even business leaders. The social media we create as individuals can make all of us instant sensations nearly overnight. Powerful personalities can emerge from the masses that may end up leading a cause, or, may give voice to the disenfranchised. Successful individuals leverage their own personality online to drive followers and encourage action.

As social media technologies personalize the experience consumers have with businesses, we – the business owner – become the obvious spokesperson for our concerns. We become the personality behind our brand. The media we create as people will illustrate our core competencies and will become the message that relates ideas about our brand, product, or service. This gives customers and associates insight into our character, our interests, our perspectives, values, and priorities as a company. Social media and social networking personifies a brand. In turn, we have the opportunity to express ourselves and engage our "audience" with announcements, proclamations, random thoughts, important news and information, personal and professional opinions, even seemingly wacky ideas. If our company appears more approachable online – easier to work with and personable – that fosters trust and builds rapport.

In the age of Groundswell, your participation matters!

George Colony, a researcher at the Forrester Marketing Group, admitted in a media interview that very few c-level executives participated in social media.[1] Three factors influence this level of participation in social media from corporate officers. One is age and the perception of technology as a productivity tool rather than a social one.[1] Another factor concerns regulatory constraints and the inability of executives to speak openly about their business.[1] And the last factor is time.[1] Beset with the task of generating four to six 140-character meaningful statements every day becomes daunting.

You can probably see where ignoring social media may depersonalize your brand and may make your company unfathomable, unreachable, and mute; if your company isn't saying anything, its not part of the ongoing dialog between producers and consumers. Social networking is a shift from traditional marketing where the officers of a company become its celebrities or evangelists. You ignore your audience (your community) at your own peril. If your customers are increasingly expecting to engage your company online, your absence or silence could be – at best – a missed opportunity.

"You're not participating," said Colony. "That's not a follower-centric model. Many people have a lot of activity to create followers... to have a zero social profile is going to be difficult... I think boards are going to be looking for people who can be social."[1]

Social networking promotes a cult of personality around the owner/CEO. You could look at that as especially tedious and try to farm it out to somebody but then you're missing the point. Customers are trying to get closer to you and not a mouthpiece, most can see through that ruse, and the legitimacy of the executive can be compromised. You should look at social media as a regular extension to your word-of-mouth marketing as a champion of your own products and services, and even a process to tie them together.

"I would predict that more executives will see [social networking] as an opportunity rather than a risk," said Livestrong CEO Doug Ulman, himself a social media advocate.[2] "Transparency and authenticity are two important factors and social media allows us to amplify both in a significant way." [2]

Mobility

Quick: can you name the most important technology of the last decade?

Okay, well, it should have been the smart phone. World-wide, smart phone sales have out-paced notebook and computer sales; in developing nations, the smart cell phone is the principle means of using the Internet. And in western countries, the smart phone has electronically tethered us to our work, interests, hobbies, passions, and community no matter where we are.

Now think of the recent introduction of netbooks, digital pads and tablets, and ebook readers, apps, and instant messaging. Increasingly, the importance of the desktop computing platform to the business strategy of companies like Microsoft, Apple, Facebook, or Google is diminishing, while the importance of mobile computing platforms is rocketing skyward. It should come as no surprise that the future of business is directly related to a consumer expectation for mobility.

I couldn't say enough about how mobility extends our ability to be social and how social media thrives off of mobile technology. Mobility enables interconnectedness and participation by releasing us from the bonds of our desk, staring at a computer screen, waiting for the world outside to pass us by. Convergence is one thing but if we can use digital devices to communicate and share everywhere, then there's a real transformative power there because we can be both interconnected and invested in the world. We can be in the middle of a rock concert and share that experience with others. We can be in the midst of a corporate event and share that experience with our customers.

Further, businesses can leverage mobility by encouraging consumers to swing by, "badge-in", be a part of an experience onground and at your store during an event, a product release, or even a business convention. Mobility can help bring customers to you. Social media being designed around mobile technology are creating games out of being out-and-about and connected. Points can be awarded for visiting commercial locations, stats can be maintained on vast virtual dashboards, and coupons and discounts can be earned by just showing up.

And mobility is even more important to younger generations.

Interconnectedness and Participation

Think about the youngest generation of consumers entering the marketplace. They're referred to as Millineals. You've seen your kids. They have never known a time where everything understood to mankind isn't available at their fingertips, or, where their friends aren't immediately accessible. They are just as comfortable texting mindlessly as they are talking to a friend IRL (In Real Life), and disconnection and non-participation in their ongoing dialog puts them into a state of anxiety.

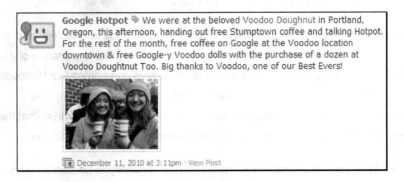

Google Hotpot 🖈 We were at the beloved Voodoo Doughnut in Portland, Oregon, this afternoon, handing out free Stumptown coffee and talking Hotpot. For the rest of the month, free coffee on Google at the Voodoo location downtown & free Google-y Voodoo dolls with the purchase of a dozen at Voodoo Doughnut Too. Big thanks to Voodoo, one of our Best Evers!

December 11, 2010 at 3:11pm · View Post

In their cultural experience, digital connectedness and participation isn't just obligatory it's mandatory - their absence from which could spell social ostracism! Gen-X, Gen-Y, and Baby Boomers may not have the same social compulsions but they have come to embrace the economies-of-scale and convenience the technology has to offer. And don't discount seniors who – as I write - comprise of the largest growth demographic in social media. Community breeds participation, especially when grandma wants to keep tabs on what the grandkids are doing, and I'm pretty sure your parents have already asked for your Facebook page. Interconnectedness and Mobility makes updates and participation real-time; the importance of Trusted relationships can be extended into the moment of now - tapping top-of-mind-awareness.

The Long Tail and Free

Chris Anderson is the Senior Editor of Wired Magazine and wrote two very successful books by the same titles late in the last decade. In his book *The Long Tail*, Anderson looks at the statistical curves of consumption and argues that more money can be made promoting the obscure 80-percent of a catalog than the popular 20-percent of the same catalog. Because of the profit motive, the costs of distribution, reproduction, or warehousing, mass media has always introduced a bias to promote products desired only by popular demand by sacrificing shelf-space for what relatively fewer consumers want. As a business owner, you're likely only to carry on your shelves what's likely to sell, right, and not some obscure product that may only turn-over one unit in a year?

The Long Tail looks at the way the Internet can offer consumers the hard-to-get, obscure 80-percent of a catalog in a cost-effective way. Marketing efforts can be transformed to promote what's found in the tail of the curve and not what's found at the head of the curve; there's more money and more sales to be had in the bottom 80-percent than in the top 20-percent.

And in *Free*, Anderson looks at how digital and electronic inventories afford a zero-marginal cost for storage, replication, and distribution so that producing just one unit is equal to producing a million, continuously driving down prices to a point where products could nearly be given away for free, or, in return for recurring subscription revenue – potentially redefining business as we understand it.

So what do I mean by Free?

A good friend of mine was looking at my business model and – in particular - my commercial website and he was just astounded. He had glanced at all of my online presentations, videos, articles, and nearly 500 blog posts. "You're giving all of this information away for free. How are you making any money?"

And that's when I had to explain Free to him, too.

Information in our digital economy is abundant. It's not a scarce resource like it used to be and consumers expect to see information abundantly at no cost; from apps to cell phones, from advice to information, Free is expected.

He was really taken aback by this. What I was telling him was that information in an Information Age is abundant, and people would expect information as they expect water ... well, Free.

Then I went through a couple of ideas with him:

- **Free helps the buying decision.** Providing relevant information is important to me as a consultant because it demonstrates my competencies, background, and opinion on certain strategies.

- **Free is a great marketing and visibility strategy.** Potential clients can look at my Free stuff and get a feel for my expertise and approach to my work. Everything I add to my website as content exists in the Long Tail – words, ideas, and phrases build more relevance for my brand, making it easier for people to find me on search engines. Without a cost-based barrier to entry, it's easier to do business with me.

- **Free is costless.** It used to be that sharing information wasn't Free. It was expensive. Now, it's costless. I can throw gigabytes of material into a public space and distribute it to millions of people for practically nothing.

- **Free builds an audience of potential customers.** If more people stumble across my work and like what I do, and if they "LIKE" my Facebook page or "Friend" me in social media, then that's a good thing. That's a subscriber to my channel – to my brand – somebody interested in what I've got to say.

- **Free is a competitive differentiator.** If somebody goes to a competitor of mine and just sees an inventory of services and pricing, how does the absence of Free information diminish the relationship? The consumer may not feel as if they're adequately informed. They may not feel closer to that party because they can't see or hear them. They may even feel alienated and skeptical of what they're seeing on the web – maybe this guy can't deliver?

Free, in the new economy, is essential. It builds trust and helps the consumer try something without a scary commitment, without a barrier to entry, making it easier to do business with you. Without leveraging Free, businesses in the new economy are at a real disadvantage. They're comparatively less-transparent, more expensive, and consumers don't know who they are.

Groundswell and the effects of digital media are forces shaping Long Tail and Free dynamics. The voice of the customer is more powerful than ever and increasingly those voices desire access to the most obscure and not the most popular. Whether it's ideas, blogs, video, products, music, news, brands, radio or television shows – you name it – the economics of digital media means we can offer more content and capability at increasingly lower costs, and consumers have come to expect *Free*. Where content is abundant and free, niches are more increasingly more relevant.

The Long Tail and Free are forces which enable social media. We couldn't do it without them! Since social media is an alternative to mass media, products can thrive and prosper with relatively smaller niche audiences. Search technology and social networks help push audiences to the highest quality content in Long Tail, and long-term storage and distribution is costless. Strategically, the small business owner would consider how these forces attract the niche audience and provides extra value beyond the first financial transaction for a product or service.

Abundance Versus Scarcity

Business has historically been about managing and profiting from scarcity. If you were sitting in one of my businesses classes, I'd try to convince you that traditional entrepreneurial resources – land, labor, capital – are finite and their application costs money, and we need to earn a profit to reinvest into the business to become far more efficient at using them to create our products. If our investments allow us to reduce our costs to the lowest possible level, the rest of that profit could be returned to you or your shareholders, increasing wealth and value for the owners of the firm. Since mismanagement of this process would contribute to unacceptable levels of waste that would spell the end of a business concern, the financial controls put into place over spending, the controls represented by a hierarchy of decision-makers, and the attention spent on measuring financial returns, are all aspects of contending with the scarcity of raw material.

However, that's not necessarily the way it works now, and let's look at a few examples.

Amazon is a book store. Unlike an onground book store, they're not limited by physical constraints that surround inventory, distribution, leases, or utility expenses. They don't need a lot of labor to move around books that exists as bits. Amazon can have many millions of titles – an abundance of books – at practically zero cost for every book they add to their catalog. Amazon's business model is all about Long Tail and Abundance.

iTunes is a music store. Unlike an onground music store, they're not limited by physical constraints that surround inventory, format, or distribution. iTunes can have millions of recordings - an abundance of music – offered continuously at one very low cost and one very predictable margin, at practically zero cost for every recording, artist, or album they add to their catalog. ITunes is both successful and profitable because they leverage Abundance and Long Tail.

Netflix is a video store. Unlike Blockbuster, they're not limited to the physical constraints limiting an onground catalog to maybe 4,000 titles at sit at the head of the Long Tail – the movies and television shows that are most likely to sell and that Blockbuster would likely showcase. Instead, Netflix offers an abundance of video titles that can be browsed in the length of the Long Tail so that you can conveniently watch *The Breakfast Club* and *Roman Holiday* when and where it suits you. And it costs Netflix nearly nothing to offer such variety, choice, and convenience through their online interface which simply adds more value to your relationship with every transaction. Netflix is possible because of the abundance of bits and its Long Tail.

Making Sense of the Forces

Insofar we've discussed broad-spectrum forces that should have already started shifting your strategic thinking. There's an interrelationship between all of these forces that are driving the zeitgeist of social media, and the software tools that arise to attend to social media leverage these forces. Think about it:

- The purpose of Facebook is to help sustain Communities around brands and products, to create Cults of Personality, and to foster Trust with its constituents;

- The demise of Blockbuster and Hollywood Video and the rise of NetFlix is directly related to Long Tail and the Abundance of Bits;

- Twitter leverages Community, Cults of Personality, and Mobility to maintain top-of-mind-awareness about values and ideas;

- Blogging taps into Free, Abundance, and Long Tail principles, but it also works to convey expertise and to build Trust around brands;

- Businesses that throw a page up on Facebook are leveraging Groundswell so that they can listen to their Community, and are using it to help personify their brand;

- Consumers will follow brands because of Interconnectedness and Participation, and because of a desire to have a voice offered by the Groundswell, and to Trust the brands they do business with;

- YouTube leverages Free, Community, Long Tail, Cults of Personality, and Abundance;

- FourSquare puts the power of Community and Mobility together to create a game for earning privileges and promotions from companies they visit onground.

Again, I'd like to try to convince you that the tools (Twitter, YouTube, FourSquare, Facebook) are fleeting; understanding the tools is not as important as understanding the forces they exploit. Plus, the tools change all of the time. Keeping up with that change isn't very important - you can always hire expertise with a tool - but you can't design a strong social media strategy if you don't understand the underlying forces at play that shape it. I feel that if you can understand those underlying forces, I believe you can craft a stronger social media strategy for your small business.

Fear not, young Jedi: you shouldn't require a high metachlorine count to start your social media training – use the Forces, Luke!

- The reach and exposure of a small business is abundant and global;

- Connectivity is abundant and everywhere;

- Access to media, ideas, brands, products, and services is abundant and free;

- Communication, interaction, and audience is unlimited;

- Consumers expect more participation and community and engagement in their relationships with brands and products;

- Consumers expect more value from every transaction;

- Consumers get to control the narrative surrounding brands and not mass media institutions or corporations;

- And consumers are continuously using Trust as a basis to refer others to products and services.

Follow-up Questions

1. How are Groundswell principles guiding your social media strategy? How well are you listening to your customers?

2. Is there opportunity in the Long Tail and Free for your company? Can you create a set of social media content that costs you next to nothing to distribute yet creates value for your customers?

3. Who's managing your social media strategy? Are they introverted or extroverted? How will that play to your social media campaign needs?

4. Is your company adapting to a converged, social computing platform? Aren't even employee relationships inherently social? How can everything in your company be social?

5. Who are the strong personalities that are speaking on behalf of your business? How is their cult of personality shaping and personifying your brand?

6. How is your business tapping into the forces of Mobility and Interconnectedness? Are there ways to constantly be in-touch with your audience even while they're away from the desktop computer? If a customer was right outside your door, what would you say to them to invite them in?

7. Is your company still operating in a Scarcity model? How can it shift to an Abundance model? How can it leverage these forces to transform itself and to survive in a more competitive economy?

8. Is Trust, Transparency, and Authenticity at the very heart of your social media strategy? Why not? Isn't that good for both employees and for consumers?

9. How would you describe the values of your business? What are the top three things your business stands for? If you can't answer that question off-the-bat, neither can your customers.

10. Are you too focused on the number of LIKES from your Facebook campaign, instead of unifying customers around your values and ideas?

References

1. Dybwad, Barb. *Should CEO's be Fluent in Social Media?* Interview. Found on the World Wide Web on August 12, 2010. URL: http://mashable.com/2010/04/23/should-ceos-be-fluent-in-social-media-interview/

2. Van Grove, Jennifer. How CEO's will use Social Media in the Future. Found on the World Wide Web on September 7, 2010. URL: http://mashable.com/2010/08/30/ceo-social-media-future/

3. Kessler, Sarah. January 13, 2011. HOW TO: Create a World-Class Online Community for Your Business. Found on the Internet on January 15, 2011. URL: http://mashable.com/2011/01/12/online-community-business/

Part Three
What You Will Learn

- An introduction to the kinds of technologies employed by social media

- How these technologies can be used by a small business

- How we use these technologies to relate ideas, words, and concepts to our brand

- How we build traffic to our Destination through the use of social networks and social bookmarking

- How a small business can use these tools to tap into the Groundswell

Social Media Tools

In my consulting practice, I like to deal with broad classifications of technology to make them easier to understand and social media comprises of an abundance of technology so I like to categorize and generalize about them. There are so many and they perform so many different (if not redundant) functions that many business owners I meet are quickly overwhelmed and they're so intimidated by the breadth of social technology that's available that they never get started.

Yet some are little bit more gutsy. Maybe they'll take some advice from a 14 year-old grandson and open a Twitter account. At a leadership conference, they could've been taught how to use Facebook to create a profile page. Unfortunately, they're educated on function yet ignorant on purpose: neither of these example business owners really understands how the technology works for them, how it can be measured, how it could be used, or how much attention should be paid to it.

We've already discussed Free and it's an important principle at play with social media. Software that drives social media and social networking is free. That's part of its attraction in that anyone can participate, regardless of computing platform, geography, income level, or computer knowledge. Social media is open to the public - anywhere and everywhere. All it takes is the software and an Internet connection.

Before we begin, a word of warning. Many people get hung up on the tool assuming that the tool is the end-all-to-be-all. Don't. Tools are just tools. Tools come and go. They come in a variety of forms and are constantly evolving. As a technology consultant, I really try to remove the complexity and stigma surrounding these tools so that they're understood as broader instruments to carry off your plan. If you need help with the tool and you haven't the time nor inclination to learn how to use it, hire someone. They're not important for you (the strategist) to know.

Here's a quick-run down of the tools we'll be talking about next.

- Websites

- Search Engines (Google, Yahoo!, Bing)

- Blogs

- Podcasts and Vidcasts

- Microblogs (Twitter, Flickr)

- Feeds and Aggregators (RSS, Google Reader)

- Social Search (Facebook, Linked-In)

- Social Bookmarking (stumbleupon, del.icio.us, digg, reddit, newsvine)

- Tagging

- Social Networks (Facebook, Linked-In)

- Location-Based (Mobile) Networking

Websites (Destinations)

Websites allow small businesses to leverage Long Tail and Abundance.

What You Need to Know

- A website is an online Destination where your brand and company can be found

- Effective business websites extend value through self-services and information

- A website should demonstrate and elaborate upon your core competencies

- Business websites must encourage consumers to act

Description

There's nothing really extraordinary about owning a website on the Internet. Many small businesses already have a website even before engaging in a social media strategy. Still, I find that many small business owners don't understand the rationality behind owning a website – they know that they must have one but they aren't clear what it's doing for their business. In a few simple terms, let me explain why you need a website and why owning one relates to social media.

- **Websites create a Destination on the web.** This is a location for your business - a presence on the web – that allows you to promote your products and services. I will often refer to your website as your Destination on the web. It is your web property: a virtual storefront working for you around the clock. Your website represents your brand and the value you bring to every customer. Your website is a repository for content that gets related to your brand. It's where people go to find information about your company and to do business with you.

In many ways, your website is the first impression that consumers have of your business and its appearance is a determining factor of whether or not they intend to work with you. Consider:

- *How does your website reflect your business and its core competencies?*

- *How should your website change to reflect your current branding and target audience?*

- *If your Destination is speaking for you while you're not around, what is it saying?*

- **Websites are a sales and leads channel.** A small businesses mightl look at their website as a sales channel because they've e-commerce products that are sold online. Other businesses look at their site as a means to generate sales leads by encouraging the consumer to call the company or to use a contact us form. Either way, it's common practice for business owners to track the source of leads to best understand how their online Destination contributes to the bottom-line. If you're not already aware of those ratios (the percentage of leads and sales generated by your website as compared to other channels), you will want to understand those numbers prior to launching your social media strategy. Consider:

  - *If you're unaware of your sales channels and how business is generated from them, how will you know if your social media strategy has been successful?*

  - *In what ways does your website make it easy to Convert a visitor – generate a sale, contact your sales team, or make a commitment to call you? How does your site make it easier to do business with you?*

  - *Visitors to your website are quickly looking for information that qualifies you as an expert. They're looking for what makes you different from your competitors. How does your website currently express this?*

- **Websites provide your Visitors with self-service tools.** Consider your web Destination a place where customers can interact with you even while you're not around, and to the extent that they can self-service their relationship with you – essentially interact with your company electronically over your website –

you can curtail the cost of your growth. Instead of taking routine service calls, consumers could solve their own problems with web-based tools and automation; instead of expending your labor to answer routine questions, consumers are able to download a document, or, have a question answered online for them. Consider:

- *How is your website helping you extend value in your business relationships?*

- *How does the website shift your labor expenses to self-service functions? How does it reduce time for your customer?*

- *How does your website address routine questions and problems that are frequently encountered in your business model? Either internally to your staff or externally to stakeholders and customers?*

- **Websites provide legitimacy.** If you consider that 85-percent of all consumers first turn to an Internet search engine to find a local business, and search engines direct consumer traffic primarily to websites, then your website is the Destination you want these customers to see. Your website provides proof of your existence. It's also the first layer in your sales strategy that helps direct the consumer to take action and to contact you. Consider:

  - *What does a poorly-designed, incomplete, or inaccurate website say about your company's credibility?*

  - *If your website isn't communicating expertise and experience in your field, how is it working to help convince the customer to work with you?*

  - *If your website doesn't differentiate you from your competitors, what will drive the customer to contact you?*

- **Websites create a repository for curated content.** Websites are the online container where we'll add more and more information in to. When a website is first launched, it's an empty bucket. We slowly add a little more content – a blog post here, a video there, another blog post, perhaps a podcast the following week - to help explain our core competencies. Then we add a little more. And then a little more. We provide presentations, white papers, FAQ's (Frequently Asked Questions), online services, testimonials, pictures of our best work, video, and our vision, mission, and ideas. Over time, we've amassed a collection of ideas that relate back to our brand, products, and services. Our Destination is the place where we put all of this electronic content so that it can be available to anyone our Long Tail. Consider:

- *If you're not curating content and the information about your business is stale, how does that reflect upon your brand? Upon first impressions when Visitors find you online?*

- *Is your website simply a brochure and contact form? How are your competitors using video, presentations, social media, or interactive tools to help explain their services and land the sale?*

- *If your website is never updated, then in Internet-terms, it becomes increasingly irrelevant and more difficult for consumers to find. When's the last time new, fresh ideas (content) were added to your website?*

- **Websites are a honeypot for spiders.** Because your website is a Destination where all of your content lives on the web, we want spiders – automated programs dispatched by search engines that seek out information on the Internet and relate it back to websites – to crawl your site and relate these ideas back to your website and your brand. As bees are attracted to honey, spiders are attracted to new content. The better your website is at attracting spiders, the greater relevance you have online. Consider:

- *Is your website broken? If your website has a lot of technical problems like missing links, this prevents your website from being indexed or read by the spider. This could hurt your visibility on search engines.*

- *How are the keywords on your website relevant to what you do, and how people will find you online?*

- *When is the last time you discussed Search Engine Optimization (SEO) with your web developer?*

Call-to-Action

Destinations should have a clear call-to-action. What do you want the visitor to do?

- Should they call your company?

- Fill out a form?

- Download a white-paper?

- Print a coupon?

- Visit your online store with a promotion code?

- Come participate in an event at your store?

- Learn about your products or services?

- Engage in a discussion?

- Sign-up for your webinar?

- Join your mailing list?

- Subscribe to your newsletter?

You see, the problem with many small business websites is that they're generally ineffective at convincing the customer to do anything. So the visitor comes around, looks at the site, perhaps reads an article, then doesn't see much of interest, entertainment, or a call-to-action, and then they leave. A very unsatisfactory experience that didn't compel them to do anything isn't what we're after. We want to immediately strike the visitor's imagination, interest, or action, and compel them to do something when they visit. All Destinations should have a clear call-to-action.

A Word on Website Design

Now that we understand some of the strategic benefits surrounding a website, it should be obvious to you that the effectiveness of your Destination is key to your marketing success. Arguably, it's the most important factor of this problem: a social media campaign simply builds off of the capabilities of a strong online Destination; it's the foundation for everything.

Having a well-designed, technically-clean, updated website, however, is only the first step in preparing a social media strategy. The website is the reflection of your company and its brand on the Internet. It's your Destination – the place that your social media efforts will drive traffic to.

In terms of design, websites can be complicated or they can be simple but they instantly convey the image of your brand to a potential consumer. If they're too simplistic that a potential customer may not take you seriously; if they're too complicated, a potential customer may be turned off by the difficulty of finding what they're looking for. A website is an exercise in good function as much as beautiful design.

A website is integral to a social media marketing campaign because it is your Destination. It is a web property that represents almost everything a potential customer would need to know to engage in business with you. If anything else, your brand must have a presence on the web that's accessible by everyone. The website is the cornerstone that allows you to convey ideas and information to potential consumers everywhere.

It was quite fashionable to own your own web site when the Internet was for started. This meant hiring and retaining a web developer on your staff because developing web pages was technically challenging. Around 2000, this expectation changed where most web development is done on a contract basis; it is unusual for companies these days to hire and retain their own web developer unless their competency demanded it. Even still, it was necessary to have a relationship with a web developer so that changes could be uploaded to the site, and a developer was necessary to improve Search Engine Optimization (SEO) because only they understood the arcane laws that surrounded search engines.

Yet, as we enter the next decade in 2010, this expectation has changed once again. Web sites have now become complex applications and data bases called

Content Management Systems (CMS). Once setup, the CMS can be manipulated entirely by an end user without much intervention from a web developer.

Content management systems are modular and can support an array of automated features that are easy even for an end user to install. CMS's can save a company big bucks by transferring daily management to internal resources since it affords them the flexibility to add and remove content on their own. And all content is automatically optimized by CMS for search engines. A CMS removes all of the mystery and complexity of websites, making them simple to update and maintain.

I try to encourage all of my small to mid-range businesses to adopt Content Management Systems so that they can own and manage their website themselves.

Destinations are a repository for curated content. Destinations offer an opportunity to help curate content over time. This is content that your company has hand-crafted, picked, selected, and has made available for public consumption. Your Destination is a library of ideas that you've deemed so important to relate it to your brand and services. If you think about it, managing content on a Destination isn't just an effort of creating but of managing over time. Curators manage content in a constant process of making it easier to collect, sort, find, use, organize, and distribute; of showcasing old content in new ways; of presenting old ideas in perhaps new context. Even old information that's been deposited in the curated collection may still be of some interest and that's why we try to make it available in our Long Tail.

Search Engines
Search Engines helps find content in the Long Tail.

 Without Search, Are You Real?

What You Need to Know

- Search engines are private tools that help find everything on the web.
- Programs called spiders crawl the web to look for new online content.
- Content found by spiders are indexed and are related back to your brand.

- Content (keywords, concepts, and ideas) found on your website should be easily crawled so they can be related back to your Destination.

Examples

- Google
- Bing
- Yahoo!
- Ask

Description

So which one do you think came first: the website or the search engine? They're both so totally intrinsic to each other that they're difficult to separate. Well, when web technologies were being developed for teletype machines in the 1960s, nobody ever thought about trying to find information on an interconnected network of computers. The assumption was that you, as a systems person, would know where something was, otherwise you'd have no business looking at it in the first place.

Even after 30 years of development, when the modern Internet made its debut in the 1990's, there was still no native way to direct people to resources on the Internet. In order for you to know where a Destination was found on the Internet, you had to go to other sites that maintained lists of new web pages and linked to them. Without automation, these indexes were maintained by hand and given the rapid growth of the Internet, it became increasingly difficult to manage all of those lists. So the Internet was itching to have a technology developed to help find all of those new web pages.

Many private parties experimented with ways of categorizing, filtering, and listing web pages on the Internet. What resulted from that era were topical and categorized indexes of websites, but it wasn't very easy to search all of their content nor determine which content was most related to what you were looking for. It wasn't until Google's 1998 release that the modern search engine came of age.

Since then, the search engine has become an essential tool for finding practically anything on the Internet.

In today's interconnected online marketing environment, few things are more important to understand than the mechanics of search engines; social media, in fact, builds-upon the technologies that drive them. So briefly, I'd like to take just a few moments to explain how they work.

The search engine is a giant card catalog with over 20 billion entries experiencing tens of millions of daily updates. Yikes! Imagine the size of that catalog if it were on paper and the army of people you'd need to manage it. To consumers, search engines are a trusted advisor, faithfully finding and directing them to content they're interested in. Meanwhile, to businesses, the search engine is a referral partner. Search engines are the way that consumers' interests are matched to potential service providers in their local area.

Mechanically, search engines are comprised of just four main components: a database, a spider, an index, and an algorithm. All modern search engines generally work in the same way.

A search engine's **database** is a monstrously-large repository of information related to websites. Data maintained in these databases has to be very quickly provided to meet consumer expectations – nobody has the patience to wait more than a few seconds for search engine results - and that demands an extraordinary amount of processing power, storage, and memory, so they're expensive and complicated to run.

An **index** is a relationship built between the ideas and websites. The linkages between ideas, pictures, music, files, and where they can be found are maintained by these indexes. Indexes are the main way that a search engine knows what web sites to return if it were asked a question.

Content on the Internet is constantly changing. It would be nigh-impossible for even that army of human beings we mentioned earlier to constantly monitor 20 billion web pages for changes and manually update the search engine's database, and that poses an enormous engineering problem: how do you maintain the accuracy of a database of information so big and so variable? The answer to that problem was a search engine spider.

Spiders are programs dispatched by search engines to enumerate content. Spiders crawl from one web site to another web site by following hyperlinks. Crawling is done every second, every minute, every hour, and every day. Spiders never get tired because they're programs. When the spider comes to a web site, it gathers up approximately 250 words of text per page and some other relevant information that describes that page, and then it writes what it finds to the big database used by the search engine. After it's done, the spider will crawl another hyperlink found on the page, consume another 250 words of text, record the time and date, and copy that information back to the big database again. This process is ceaseless.

After a while, indexes are rebuilt against these databases creating new relationships between content and websites found by the spiders. But where's the intelligence? How does a search engine like Google know that I'm looking for Red Sox (the baseball team) versus information on "red socks"?

That's all due to the **algorithm**: the proprietary way that a search engine makes sense of all the data found in an index. It's really complicated but a search algorithm applies a bunch of tests that takes what you're searching for and compares it to the most popular destinations on the Internet; Google, for example, uses well over 200 separate relevance factors for each website it gives back to you so that it's the most meaningful to your question.

Search engine components are a pretty well-understood technology. Databases, indexes, and spiders are an industry-wide phenomenon. What isn't completely understood and what gives a search engine its uber-unique power to find what you're looking for is the search algorithm: the formula needed to match a single abstract idea against 20 billion (and growing!) possibilities. And nobody's algorithm is better than Google's. It's search algorithm is the core intellectual property that gives it a $199 billion market cap and a 72% market share.

Search is a nuanced business and there are plenty of books out there on maximizing the search effectiveness of your website. Generally, however, let me impart five basic Search pointers that aren't difficult to understand and can help improve your Destination's visibility substantially on the Internet:

1. **Keyword Lists.** Maintain a list of 20 keywords, phrases, or core ideas about your company. The list should be shared with your Storytellers (see Part 5). These words would be used frequently and often – consistently – to help describe your brand in all forms of social media.

2. **Three Levels Max.** Critical content (product information, contact information, etc.) should be no further than three levels from the main page of your website. That makes for more likely indexing by the spider.

3. **Content Management System (CMS).** Talk to your web developer about implementing a CMS like WordPress or Drupal. Systems like these provide for a technically-convenient, simple, and effective site processing by spiders.

4. **Blogging Should Reinforce Products.** Concepts and ideas used in your social media campaign should often refer to products and services that you offer, and if you have a trademarked product name, referring to that name often like a keyword would be a great idea.

5. **Backwards-Link Always.** Your social media should provide links back to Funnels (see Part 4) that compel the customer to act. All of your email, faxes, all correspondence in print or digital form should somehow reference your Destination.

So by this point, the importance of a well-designed, frequently-updated Destination on the Internet may be starting to resonate with you.

*   Stale information found on a web site is glossed over by spiders
*   Spiders feel that infrequently updated information is less relevant than fresh information

- Web sites that are broken or have technical problems aren't read by spiders which means the content doesn't get indexed and can't be seen by search engines
- If spiders collect the wrong ideas and relate them to your website, that could be very bad
- Websites that aren't designed well aren't read well by spiders
- More Long Tail content means more opportunities for spiders to relate ideas to your website
- Spiders believe your website is more authoritative if other websites link back to it
- Spiders don't chew well on pictures or video – they only understand text; too many pictures and video aren't useful to conveying information to the spider

Understanding the relationship between Search and your Destination is extraordinarily important in attracting new customers in a world of increasing competition and near infinite choice.

Blogging
Blogging leverages Trust, Cults of Personality, Free, Long Tail, and Abundance.

 How to Bring More Visitors to Your Blog

What You Need to Know

- Blogging is the practice of writing about your competencies as a business.

- Keywords, ideas, and concepts articulated in Blogs are crawled by spiders, indexed, and are related back to your Destination.

- Frequent updates of content provided via Blogging are attractive to spiders and makes your Destination appear more important, improving your search engine rankings.

- Blogging presents an opportunity to differentiate yourself from your competitors and personalize your brand.

Examples

- WordPress

- Blogger

- Drupal

- Livejournal

Description

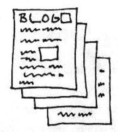

A blog – a concatenation between the words "web-based log" – is a common social media tool used to convey the thoughts, ideas, opinions, and experiences of the writer. Anyone can create a blog. Anybody *can* blog. Blogs had a humble beginning: they were nothing more than web pages on the Internet until social media came around which allowed anyone to create and maintain one. Today, there are millions of Blogs and subsequently millions of bloggers constantly writing about a vast array of topics. In the last few years, blogs have gained significant readership and even contend with traditional media outlets for delivering news and information.

Blogging is the act of writing a blog. A vast majority of these blogs are hobbies and enthusiast work that do not generate a professional income. Many bloggers write blogs purely out of the sense of satisfaction they receive from sharing something they're passionate about. Very few blogs are actually maintained on a regular basis, generate a livable wage for its author, or become the sole writing outlet for the author.

Companies will use blogs to illustrate how the company solves problems; it can also be used to express the ideas and opinions of the company's management or line level employees. Blogs help convey the personality of a company as much as it helps illustrate how the company provides value to its customers.

Businesses will use blogs as a showcase for case studies. Customers that visit the blog can learn more about the company and its services through stories that are told. If you think about it, that's what customers are really after: to hear stories about how you helped a customer and solved their problems. People really relate to stories and that's where good business blogging works – by telling a story.

Fundamentally, though, a blog is used by a business to create Long Tail content. Material ideas that hang around on your website for a long time, that can be read by spiders, and that can relate those ideas back to your brand.

Like we've discussed, content is very important to being seen on the Internet. The more content you have that contains the keywords relative to your business, the easier it is for search engines to relate those ideas to your website. If you are blogging frequently about washing dogs and providing pictures and narrative describing the act of washing dogs, and you run a dog wash, you can see how easy it is for the search engine to connect the idea of "washing a dog" to your company. You're blogging about it all of the time. Google thus believes you must be an authority.

As a business, you would want the blog to be integrated with your company's web site so that ideas concerning your subject matter can be easily-related back to your brand. A blog is a critical piece of your Destination on the web.

Some of the business owners I talk to are naturally hesitant. "Writing an article several times a week?", they ask. "How will I find time to do that?" In their head, they're picturing blogs as a magazine that has a formal journalistic style, a certain composition and length requirement, and a professional author style.

Well, that's not really how blogs work. Blogs are the most perfect when they're imperfect – that is to say, when they're reflecting human emotions and expressions. That's when they're the most *authentic*. Some bloggers only write a couple of sentences a day and are very successful; some may write two or three paragraphs a week; some blogs may only contain pictures of clients, customers, or events; all of them though are written to reflect a personality, or, a point of view. Blogs are informal means of communication and work by reaching out to customers on a more intimate level.

Successful business Blogs are characterized by four things: frequency, length, perspective, and comments.

In terms of frequency, search engines look at websites as being more relevant if they have frequent updates and changes. Search engines believe that inactivity is less relevant, so the most successful blogs are updated with some regularity. And people are like this, too. If your readership doesn't see any activity from you over the course of a week they're less inclined to pay attention and read your posts. Frequency is important but this does not have to be daily. Two times a week is sufficient for a business blog; once a week is a little too thin.

Length is not as bad as you might think it is. The most optimum length for a blog post is 250-300 words. Any more than that is ignored by the search engine. Still, 250 words is a lot of narrative to parse through if you're a reader of blogs, so many blog authors would encourage you to write in a quick, short, bursty style that's easy to read and be acted upon; bullets or lists can be easily skimmed; something with a strong lead to catch their attention and a stronger conclusion that compels an action, or, with a tip that the reader could apply today. If you're writing more than 300 words at one sitting it's somewhat counterproductive. Spiders won't pay attention to the narrative after 300 words and you're likely losing your audience midway through your piece as they haven't the patience to read the entire narrative.

Finally, comments are feedback messages posted by users who read your blog. Comments generally arrive in one of three forms: comments may be constructive atta'boys appreciating your content, comments may be degrading and scathing slander hating your content, or comments may be spam. To search engines, comments of all types are a good thing; the spider tends to think more comments equals an interactive audience and that you had something meaningful to say. To you, though, some of the material posted as comments may be obnoxious, insulting, or inappropriate; your blog will allow you to delete them if you so choose.

A couple of simple ideas to get started with business blogging:

1. The business blog should be a part of the company's website.

2. The total amount of words in a single blog post shouldn't exceed 300.

3. New posts should be done at least twice per week; three times if it could be managed.

4. A regular posting schedule should be maintained throughout each week.

5. In addition to text, videos and pictures are extraordinarily powerful in conveying expertise. Use a paragraph of text to help explain the pictures and video.

6. Attention should be paid to grammar, style, and aesthetics - the blog, what it says, and how it's said represents your company and its brand. Treat it with respect.

7. Assign a regular author or set of contributors who will be responsible for blog content; it be great if these individuals were also responsible for the social media marketing campaign.

8. Try not to sell. Instead, tell a story. Convey your experience. Provide a testimonial. Give the customer some useful information they could apply today.

9. Personify and be authentic. People want to do business with you because they like you and they like what you have to say. Blogs are relatively informal mediums and shouldn't read like a memorandum or a sales brochure.

10. Always reply to every comment made on a blog - even if it's negative - and think the contributor for their time. Show your readers that you're listening. You might even take the time to describe how you'll correct a problem. Blogs are a two way medium. Take advantage of that.

So that's the connection between a company's Destination and blogging, whereas blogging is used to maintain relevance and gain increasingly higher positions in search engine results. Blogging is one of the most common, easiest, and most cost-effective ways to engage in social media.

Podcasts and Vidcasts

Podcasts and Vidcasts tap into Free, Abundance, Mobility, Interconnectedness, and Long Tail.

What You Need to Know

- Both are conceptually related to Blogging although comparatively both are more technically-difficult to produce and distribute than Blog content.
- Video and audio mediums allow you to convey many complex problems far easier than in narrative, and it's portable – people can listen to audio content in a car, for example.
- Video and audio can help personify your brand.
- Vidcasts and Podcasts don't displace the use of a Blog, rather they expand upon ideas presented in a Blog and encourages more thought or engagement from an audience.

Description

Both of these kinds of media could be thought of as a miniature radio show or television show produced on a microcomputer and distributed across social media. Their convenience as a medium couldn't be more apparent: both integrate seamlessly into portable digital devices like iPods and make it easy for consumers to bring this media along with them on the road, and listen to it while they're driving or traveling.

Podcasts are audio recordings that are produced with an introductory sound-track and a concluding footer soundtrack, and in-between is what could be characterized as a radio program. Content may include how-to's, interviews, opinion pieces, reviews, or tips. They're created with software on a personal computer and saved into a format that can be listened to on many common digital devices, and then distributed through RSS Feeds (explained further on in Part Three). The 'pod' part of the 'cast' comes from the ubiquity of Apple's iPod product and its relationship to downloading and listening to content like this from all across the Internet. Vidcasts are pretty much the same thing except they're video productions.

At the center of a well-produced podcast or vidcast is a personality. There must be a clever, distinctive voice behind the podcast that drives interest and maintains the audience's attention. I can't think of anything worse than listening to a dull, droning voice in my car for longer than a minute. The personality could be a real person or a persona created for the purpose of producing the podcast. Talent can be found internally or externally to a company, but there should be a very prominent, continuous, interesting personality that drives the show and its message. It's the personality that keeps subscribers hooked.

Podcasting and Vidcasting aren't *simple* and I was hesitant for even bringing them up given the title of the book. Their production and distribution is actually quite technical and can be a complicated endeavor, but there again, expertise can be sought-out that can help with those aspects of the medium. They both suffer from the same issue I mention in the video and pictures section of the book regarding amateur versus professional appearances: a poorly-produced podcast could damage a brand just as efficiently as a well-produced vidcast could jump-start one. Great care and consideration should go into their development.

If there are any ideas I could impart on this subject, here are just a few common-sense concepts for the business podcaster:

- Keep both types of casts between 3 minutes and 6 minutes; this is an adequate window of time to be able to convey a message while not boring the audience beyond ten minutes.

- Since the medium is a serial subscription-based production, extra content could easily be off-loaded into future releases and editions.

- Feature interviews of prominent people in your industry, company, or even customers. Rotate new voices into the program to keep it interesting.

- Solicit engagement and feedback from the listening audience in the form of voicemail, then, replay that voicemail back into the show and respond to the listener. This format offers a unique way to be able to listen and respond to customers. Try to leverage it.

- Partnered interview formats work very well in this medium, too; just like radio disc jockeys have side-kicks, your podcast personality needs a foil. Listeners identify with the side-kick.

- Use the podcast and vidcast to reinforce content introduced earlier in the week on your blog or on your social networking site. Use the show as a means to reinforce concepts that have already been explored. This will also drive more traffic back to your Destination as listeners will want to find resources, engage in dialog, or catch-up on content they may have missed.

- Personality is everything in this medium. Make sure there are some strong, creative, and extroverted personalities hosting the show and promote those individuals in the social media campaign.

- Consider professional production if talent isn't immediately available to you.

Microblogging

Microblogging exploits Free, Abundance, Mobility, Interconnectedness, and Long Tail.

What You Need to Know

- Microblogging distributes short, bursty messages to an audience like an alert.
- The alert can come in the form of text, pictures, audio, or video.
- An audience subscribes to receive your messages because they want to receive breaking news about your brand/company/products.
- Microblogging links to content found on your Destination – say new Blog, Podcast, or Vidcast updates – and encourages your audience to read, listen, or watch.

- Spiders also crawl microblogging platforms; more links to your Destination makes it appear more important and improves your website's search engine rankings.
- Microblogging is a means of personifying your brand.

Examples

- Twitter
- Tumblr
- Flickr
- Plurk

Description

Microblogging describes the Blogging process done in very few amount of words, pictures, or video. You're probably familiar with Twitter. Twitter is a microblogging platform. People who sign up for twitter follow others who "tweet" status updates from their computers and their cell phones. The status updates can only be up to 140 characters in length – the typical maximum length of a SMS or text message on a cell phone – and are therefore very conservative in their use of characters.

So, why microblogging?

When we are with our friends, will often share ideas in short, bursty sentences. Sometimes those ideas are funny. Sometimes those ideas are leads into another topic of conversation. Sometimes those ideas are just frivolous and may reflect our quirky sense of style or personality. Microblogging takes that fluid stream of consciousness and shares them at the speed of light to an audience of hundreds, thousands, or even tens of thousands. Everywhere.

Microblogging doesn't have to be all about words and text. Microblogging can also incorporate images and video - a great example of that is a microblogging platform called Flickr. Users load the Flickr application on their cell phones, allowing them to upload pictures taken by their phones into online photo albums that are immediately shared with their followers. Microblogs can also carry hyperlinks so that a tweet encourages somebody to click on the link and see content available on a Destination.

Now, in my opinion, fluid streams of consciousness suffer from an inherent problem of being unedited, uncensored, and excessive. Perhaps you feel the same? Using microblogging tools like Twitter often imparts a TMI-effect (too much information). You probably, for example, do not care what I just ate for lunch; you probably aren't interested in my opinion about a movie I just saw; and you may not have any interest in where I am right now. And if you follow a lot of people, you can easily become saturated in a wash of status updates that you can't possibly keep up with and end up ignoring. Further, Twitter is inundated with spammers all trying to capture your attention, too, and would very much like if you clicked on a hyperlink so it'd earn them some cash. Inasmuch, many users tend to tune out Microblogging because it's often just an overwhelming deluge of worthless information you can't do anything with.

Again, that's my opinion, and some social media experts might disagree with me but I feel that's one of the major problems associated with microblogging. There's no natural filter. The messaging is so excessive – and so much of the content is spam - that many users end up tuning out the noise.

Don't take my word for it. A study from the Pew Research Center confirms this behavior in a recent study.[1] Seventy-seven percent of Twitter users check their Twitter feed anywhere from once a day, once every couple of days, or not at all. Which is far and away from "real time". According to the Pew results, only 24% of Twitter users are actually checking their feed frequently during the day, and still most of these users are looking at very niche content - specific authors that they're interested in following.

I suppose the good news is that twitter another microblogging platforms are developing ways that make filtering and searching for updates updates easier to do. These tools are increasing and sophistication so that users can easily dissect the signal from the noise.

I tend to take a practical approach to Microblogging by looking at it as a billboard on the information highway. This relevant to businesses who are using applications like Twitter to promote their brand and who've collected a smattering of followers on a microblogging platform. Here's an example. You're driving down the freeway and you see a billboard that says, "Eat here – hamburgers for 99 cents". Now the 99¢ hamburger may very well entice you to pull off the side of the road for a quick snack because you're hungry at that exact moment. The billboard was able to tap into your subconscious concern of the moment and encouraged you to act. Microblogging is a lot like this. In just 140 characters, you appeal to your audience to pay attention to something you want to say and then provide a hyperlink back to your Destination. If a follower just happens to be looking at their Twitter feed, they might see your suggestion, find it intensely relevant, and they might feel intrigued to click on the hyperlink back to your content.

Functionally, the billboard strategy is a good way to look at using microblogging for business because it leverages top-of-mind-awareness (TOMA). Unlike any other form of media, you can deliver a short message to an attentive audience who're generally interested in your product or service, wherever they happen to be – on their computer, on their cell phone, or on a digital device like a tablet computer. There they are, working away, and Blip! Another engaging message from your brand. This is an advertising space that we all would kill for, even admittedly at the risk of turning consumers off because we're providing too much information. Successful microblogging then is a mix between leveraging TOMA to compel consumers to click back to your Destination without being so excessive as to have them ignore your updates.

1.   As a means to take the candid ideas from senior executives and put them out there for customers and investors to read, generating buzz and excitement over products and services.

2. As a means to pull consumer attention back to the company's destination.

3. Frequent updates provide top-of-mind-awareness for your company.

4. New followers from microblogging platforms can become strong business contacts or even potential customers.

5. Microblogging can be used inside an organization to provide quick answers to routine questions and to make the whole company "social". With a special hash-tag, searches off of internal tweets on Twitter could become a valuable knowledgebase.

6. Use Lists inside of Twitter to help filter content between various groups (example: employees, shareholders, experts, audience, etc.). It will help filter out the madness.

7. When considering microblogging, consider local and mobile. Where are potential consumers right now? If there anywhere near your business – if there's a special event or function – leverage Twitter to bring them closer to your doorstep.

Again, in my opinion, it's not worthwhile for a business to try and compete against the endless stream of status updates that are being routinely filtered and ignored by an audience. Instead, consumers are turning to a more palatable alternative: the social network.

Feeds
Feeds leverage Free, Abundance, Interconnectedness, and Long Tail.

What You Need to Know

*   It is helpful to imagine a Feed as a constant stream of information pulled by your audience from your website.

- Feeds are enabled by a technology called Really Simple Syndication (RSS).

- When new content is offered, it's automatically included in the Feed.

- Feeds make it easier for an audience to receive new content from your Destination; it makes it easier to consume new content offered your brand/product/service.

- Feeds are often engineered to force the user to click on a hyperlink to bring them back into your Destination to encourage visitors to come to your website.

Examples

- Really Simple Syndication (RSS)

- Google Reader

Description

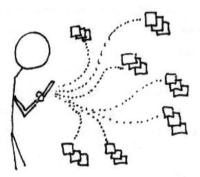

A feed refers to an Internet technology called Really Simple Syndication (RSS). An RSS feed retrieves content from websites and blogs and places them in one place that we could read those updates like email; a software we'd refer to as a RSS Reader. RSS Readers give users the ability to manage the diverse range of content we've subscribed to more efficiently than actually going to a website to view it. Using a RSS Reader is an essential time management tool for users and a practical service that'd be offered by your own website.

Feeds are form of *aggregator*. They're a way to shortcut some of the complexity associated with managing all of the new content that's published on the Internet by aggregating them – or consolidating them – into one spot. As an example, I follow a modest number of blogs and websites (around 75 of them) and it'd be very difficult for me to actually visit each site to review new content. Instead, my Google Reader pulls down new content that I'm able to review in a virtual inbox which makes reading all of the new content a little like reviewing email.

But feeds just aren't for websites. They're for you, too! Get to know Google Reader, an RSS reader tool. It's easy to find and use – just Google it. Google Reader will allow you to manage RSS subscriptions to other blogs and websites that you're interested in. It gives you a tool for managing the relevant content you're interested in from all across the web, and even your competitors.

A couple of ideas about Feeds:

1. **Content Management System.** I've said it before and I'll say it again: CMS' already has RSS feed technology built-in so it's easy to get started using Feeds if you're using one.

2. **Feedburner for Stats.** A complaint that I've always had with Feeds is that it prevents the user from visiting my Destination. They're reading a stream of my content without actually visiting my website, so I'm loosing an analytical capability to monitor first-order effects (see Part 4). Feedburner is a Google property that can be used by your web developer to create a monitored RSS feed where valuable first-order effects can be managed.

3. **Show Everything.** One of the options in providing a Feed is to truncate the content that's flowing through it as to provide incentive for users to click on a hyperlink to see the full article online, thus driving more traffic back to the Destination. Myself, I dislike that approach because it's a chore to click and open the browser to see the article. You're using Feeds to reach your audience – don't force your audience into a certain desirable behavior for you. I recommend that you set your Feeds to provide the entire article and content. It's purely a convenience issue but it also contributes to the user actually reading/viewing your content.

4. **Don't Spam.** Using Feedburner, it's possible to embed advertising into your content. I've moved away from this practice because, again, it seems insulting. I'm providing my Feed to an interested subscriber who could be genuinely interested in what I have to say, so why insult their time, interest, and intelligence by spamming them? Show your audience some dignity by omitting advertising from your Feeds. If you have advertising on your Destination, instead, try to encourage the user to visit the Destination.

5. **Participate!** Social media is social and that means you! Through subscribing to blogs and other outlets for Feeds, a RSS reader gives you an opportunity to participate and respond to others in the blogosphere (yes – that's actually a word). Start small: subscribe only to a few feeds at first – we wouldn't want to overwhelm you. When you reply to posts or engage others in discussion, don't engage in a direct sell, but demonstrate your expertise and include your tagline pointing back to your Destination. That's another backwards-facing link that improves search engine visibility, and, it could encourage others to visit your website for more information about your company, products, or services.

Preparing an RSS feed for your website is a technical exercise and one that can be best performed by your web developer. Once the feed has been created, then there is no further maintenance: every time that you post your blog or update your website, then that post is then transmitted within your RSS feed. Having a feed is important as a convenience to users so that they may easily interact with your website.

Video and Picture
Video and Pictures leverage Community and Interconnectedness.

What You Need to Know

- Studies show that consumers respond more favorably to video and pictures than text/narrative.

- Poor-quality video and pictures can damage your brand as much as good-quality content can help it.

- Video can be streamed to televisions, mobile phones, and computers – it's a very versatile medium.

- Pictures can relay visually-stunning and emotional moments that can reinforce the image of your brand, and help personify it.

- Video and pictures aren't easily indexed by spiders; special provisions must be made to relate image content to ideas that the spider can index.

Examples

- YouTube

- Google Video

- uStream

- Vimeo

Description

One of the most powerful of tools in your arsenal of social media is video. Images convey a world of ideas in a very short amount of time. The availability of inexpensive broadband connectivity has allowed video to become a marketing reality online since high-speed connections can be had by anyone, even on mobile devices. Video can be created on professional recorders or even cell phones then uploaded to sites like YouTube. Once on YouTube, a link to the video can be provided through a social network or microblogging platform, and it can even be embedded within a blog post on your Destination. The actual video file is maintained with YouTube.

Video has great economies of scale. Once a video is created it can be replayed thousands of times without incremental costs to you. Video inspires an audience; it helps personify the brand; it helps explain complex problems in a very short amount of time; it's "sticky" – visitors will watch a compelling or useful video to them. And consumers really enjoy video on mobile devices as well.

One of the most challenging aspects of video and pictures, for that matter, are that they both suffer from an obvious amateur/professionalism effect.

If you're showcasing video content on your Destination, you want to make an investment in that video from a paid videographer to produce a quality deliverable. This is particularly important if your video is featuring a prominent member of your management team. A smart, attractive, professionally-produced video that says something important about your brand in under 30 seconds is highly desirable.

However, the antithesis to that is the amateur video or – heaven forbid - the web-cam. Low-quality or budget videos without professional production will be counter-productive; dicey-looking video and picture quality could convey the wrong message about your brand, products, company, and service. You could appear much smaller than you are, or, diminish first impressions towards your company. In this way, the economies-of-scale offered by video work against you by replaying a poor image of your company a thousand times over.

There are instances where spot, quick, home-made videos work well and that's in areas of recording events or providing testimonials through your Blog. These videos are tucked-away in the Long Tail of your Destination and are available for consumption, but they're not really featured videos or a showcase about your company. They're upwards of 15-30 seconds of footage that was captured in a "raw moment" that can look more authentic to the viewer. But media such as this would rarely be featured as a highlighted form of content on your website.

My ideas concerning video and pictures:

1. **Think Quality.** Whenever possible, think about professional videography or hiring somebody with the requisite skill-set. This is the image of your business. Even a few hundred dollars can go a long way in replaying a positive, professional image of your company a thousand-times over.

2.   **Interview in Pairs.** When using video to discuss a problem with your audience, bring in an interviewer. This is somebody who is there on-script to ask a meaningful question that can then be answered by a knowledge expert from your firm. This format has been successful in media forever and allows the consumer to identify with the interviewer and their questions posed towards the expert. It's more interesting an engaging a format than just having a talking-head looking at the camera.

3.   **Keep it Short.** Remember that the average attention span of consumers on the Internet extraordinarily small. There's nothing preventing them from hitting BACK on their browser to get away from an extremely dull video. Keep your videos to under three minutes at all times; it's better to provide video in 15, 30, 45, or 60 second increments.

4.   **Keep it Real.** Videos can look highly staged and over-produced in the play-back. Strive to keep your video honest and authentic. Your audience will extend it more credibility.

5.   **Don't Create Commercials.** Instead, educate your audience on how to make a better decision; explain why they'd want your products and services over a competitor. The best kind of selling is actually just education. Try to think about the questions your customers always have and then answer those questions in the convenient form of video.

Video and pictures can be technical forms of content that's best to acquire competent resources to produce, but are extremely powerful in connecting with your customers.

Social Bookmarking

Social Bookmarking leverages Trust, Cults of Personality, Groundswell, and Community.

What You Need to Know

- Social Bookmarking is a way to allow users to vote on what the most important content is on the Web using Internet software.

- Instead of relying solely on spiders, users can indicate important content to others by bookmarking it: by classifying it and pointing to it on the Web.

- It is inherently a "geeky" activity that advocates of social media will engage in; it's not a particularly wide-spread activity among common consumers.

- Providing Social Bookmarking tools makes it easier for others to share your content, point to it, and vote on its importance.

- Social Bookmarking helps improve search engine rankings.

Examples

- Reddit

- StumbleUpon

- Digg

- del.icio.us

Description

You'll recall that search engines relate ideas and keywords back to your website. This is the primary advantage of owning a blog. The more words and ideas expressed in the blog make your website more relevant and more visible to search engines.

But keyword relationships aren't the only means that search engines use to determine relevance. Another way to determine what's important is to poll a user community through a voting process. This process is referred to as social bookmarking.

A good way to think about social bookmarking is that it gives a user the ability to vote on your content being important - much more important than others. It's a vote. And the more votes you get, the more people are suggesting that your content is some of the most important anywhere at that moment. Search engines pay attention to those results and will adjust their relevance scoring accordingly.

Technically, social bookmarking works by having a small program run on your webpage. When the button is clicked, it records the user who initiated the click, the time and date, and then publishes the hyperlink to your content to another computer on the Internet. Over time, all of these votes are tabulated and presented to users in their search results through these services.

A couple of suggestions regarding social bookmarking sites:

1. **Use just two.** Bookmarking sites are their own social network and it could be very challenging to manage more than that number. Practically, there's just not enough time in the day.

2. **But offer all of them.** On your website, you want to make it as easy as possible for others to bookmark your content. Have your web developer add all of the social bookmarking badges they can to your Destination.

3. **Use Social Bookmarking.** When you post new content to your Destination, either through the use of automation built-in to your website or through your own login to a service like digg.com or reddit.com, bookmark your content. Share it.

4. **Participate!** Use social bookmarking yourself when encountering new content on the web. Although it's a relatively time-consuming and geeky exercise, you might find it enjoyable to help curate new content on the web and share it with others.

On the web, services like stumbleupon.com, digg.com, del.icio.us, newsvine.com, and reddit.com serve as bookmarking aggregators - users can browse their websites to see what other users around the world thought were the most important news, articles, events, or ideas were of the day. Participating in social bookmarking is free and is purely an unpaid social contribution; providing a social bookmarking application on your website is yet another courtesy which helps get your content noticed.

Tagging

Tagging leverages Trust, Cults of Personality, Groundswell, and Community.

What You Need to Know

- Some content - images and video in particular - do not contain information that spiders can index very well. Therefore, well-intentioned advocates of social media will "tag" pictures and video they find on the Web.

- When they do this, they use software to add a brief description – perhaps a word or a phrase – that relates to the picture or video.

- Tags make it easier to find content online; you would provide tagging tools on your website to make it easier for others to share your content.

Examples

- Tag2Find

- Taglocity

- TagMyCloud

- TagTheNet

Description

Tagging is very similar to the idea of social bookmarking except that the end user can insert a term – usually a short word or phrase – that attaches invisibly to your content on the web. That term is referred to as a tag and a tag can then be searched upon by users to bring up all tagged websites that are related to that term. This works a little bit differently than a social bookmark in that it's not necessarily a vote but a means of categorizing content so that it can be easily searched.

Just a few ideas concerning Tagging:

1. **Your Keywords are Tags.** Remember that list of 20 keywords I advised you create for Blogging? Tags are related to Search and your Tags should reflect these keywords.

2. **Tag Your Content.** When adding new content to your Destination, you'll have the ability to describe that content through Tags. As Tags help organize and find content, you can imagine that Tagging your blog posts, photos, or video would be useful for others in locating it on your website. Tagging is a common option through your Content Management System – seek out the advice of your web developer if you get stuck.

3. **Don't Create Too Many Tags.** As a business, your Destination should be all about those 20 keywords you created earlier. Should those keywords be your Tags, don't deviate too far away from that core list. Too many Tags creates clutter and confusion over what your Destination is about. Keep it simple. Keep your Tags in alignment with your core competencies.

Tagging isn't necessarily something that the business owner should be concerned with. Your web developer will provide a means for creating and managing your own tags for your website. Tagging is another instrument of convenience that's used to help find content on the Internet and on your own website.

Social Networks

Social networking leverages Groundswelll, Trust, Cults of Personality, Community, and Interconnectedness.

Facebook Pages vs. Profiles

What You Need to Know

- Social networks represent a convergence between a computer and a communications device; that convergence has made the computer less of a productivity tool and more of a way to share, communicate, and interact with others.

- Social networks are designed around tribes – clusters of people and businesses who know each other.

- Tribes can be tapped to create extended online communities for brands, companies, and products; both consumers and producers can interact with each other; producers can directly listen to and respond to consumer feedback.

- Social networks are increasingly becoming huge data repositories of consumer data and advertising marketing tools.

- Social networks are re-defining local Search on the Internet and are making inroads to displace the importance of search engines based off personal referrals.

Examples

- Bebo

- Facebook

- Linked-In

- Plaxo

Description

So far, we've talked a great deal about the importance of owning your own Destination. We've also examined about how microblogging reaches out to a subscribed audience and compels them to come back to your Destination for fresh content. And once there, we'd love to have our audience interact with us by leaving a comment, by bookmarking our article, or by tagging our content so that it'll be easy for others to help find what you. All of these things are great. However, wouldn't it be even better if we could share our ideas with others in a large online community?

Social networks are integrated computer platforms where users can create interpersonal relationships and share their thoughts, ideas, and opinions around the world instantly. Twitter is a Microblogging platform; Facebook is a social network. There's a difference.

A social network is typified by the idea of communities and tribes. Members have shared experiences insomuch that the social network is just reinforcing everyday personal relationships that already exist. Participation and a social network is a participatory exercise in creating connections and sharing media.

 How to Link-in Like a Pro

Social networks were originally mechanisms that allowed us to easily share social media. People connected to others on social networks because they knew who they were, believed they had something interesting to say, they shared a common set of beliefs or values, or, had something relevant to share. Content that was found online could be immediately shared with others on a social network.

Over time, social networks have evolved to incorporate even larger purposes. Social networks have become the predominant means by which we receive updates from around the world, from our neighbors, from our towns and cities, as well as from our friends. Social networks have become a single gateway for news and information from official sources. Facebook – perhaps "the" social network - is only seven years old yet has redefined human relationships. At the time of this writing, over 600 million people the world-over are connected to each other using Facebook. That's a testament to the ease and convenience by which it interconnects us all. Social networking is quickly out-pacing e-mail usage among younger generations as they feel e-mail is slow and "for old people".

There are a lot of things to do on a social network. Users interact with each other by posting text, pictures, and music, and sharing that information with their friends. They'll also play competitive games with each other. Social networks are means to keep up with friends and family that you don't see on a regular basis, or a means to reconnect with others that have disappeared from your life. Social networks create and foster a sense of interconnectedness.

You've probably heard of the rule prescribed to Kevin Bacon. It's called the Six-Degree Rule? That nearly any modern Hollywood star is just six-degrees away from being connected to Kevin Bacon? This is referred to as a social network theory and marketing professionals study its effects. Marketers believe that there are just 50,000 people in the world. Only 50,000 people set the tastes, ideas, trends, and patterns that all of the other people will follow. The trick to marketing then is to reach just one of these 50,000 people who could then influence another 1,000 people connected to them. That's quite a hefty return particularly if your message was targeted to just one party.

If you're a business, the six-degree principle is tantamount to understanding how a return on investment relates to social networks. If just one person visits your content on your Destination and tags it, or bookmarks it, or posts a link to it in their social network, that one person could influence hundreds more people. And those who visit have influence over hundreds more people. What's harnessed here is an exponential affect called a network multiplier. And this is where the magic is.

Interconnections on social networks have a tenancy to create viral effects. This is to say that one person who really likes something can share it with their social network and create an exponential interest in the content. When this happens, a cascading event takes place where information is shared at instantly everywhere, and in a perfect world, your Destination – for example – is suddenly slammed by tens of thousands of visitors who're interested in your product or service. This process creates the mechanism of viral marketing within social networks. And in addition to driving traffic to your Destination, the more people who refer content in their social network will generate "buzz" - an Internet marketing term for increased brand awareness and consumer interest.

Consumers who use social networks appreciate the ability to have relationships with brands, giving rise to company pages on Facebook that allow consumers to post updates, information, videos, and questions directly to the brand. An immediacy where consumers can simply reach out and touch a brand – bringing the consumer much closer to the producer - affords a unique opportunity for the producer to interact with the consumer in a very intimate way.

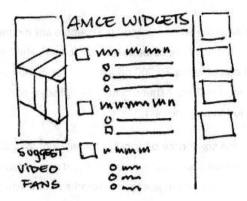

Businesses leverage the popularity and integrity of others to provide service testimonials to their friends, colleagues, family, or associates. They'll also pass along tips, ideas, and suggestions concerning their product, industry, or service. Businesses will also take the opportunity to ask its network questions about its products and services. An audience that trusts what the business has to say will forward the business' content into their own social network, granting them more exposure. Generally, the business is building off of the inherent trust found in the social network to build a base for referrals. This is a classic word-of-mouth advertising strategy.

A couple of ideas concerning Social Networks:

1. **Use Facebook.** It's the fastest-growing and most relevant platform there is. Even if you don't use Facebook exclusively and perhaps branch-out to other platforms, it's a brilliant place to start.

2. **Integrate Facebook.** There are ways that your web developer can integrate your Destination and your Facebook Page. Talk to them about it. Make it as easy as possible for your community to access and respond to your content.

3. **Linked-in and Yelp.** If you're a business professional, create a personal account on Linked-In and use it. It will become a Rolodex entry for others to find you and refer you in your professional sphere. If you're a restaurant or other entertainment establishment, consider creating a profile on Yelp. Consumer reviews on Yelp are extremely powerful.

4. **Share, Don't Sell.** A social network isn't a tool for the hard-sell. It's a great place to be able to share ideas concerning your company's core competency though.

5. **Personify.** Your voice will become the voice of your brand. Show a human face. Be authentic, genuine, and real.

6. **Advertise via Platform.** When you advertise, use the tools available to you on the platform to reach a targeted and specific audience. Facebook, for example, has a sophisticated ad program for web-based viewers, but also a location-based program called Facebook Deals. Explore these tools and factor them into your social media campaign strategy.

Another value of social networks to business relates to the potential advertising tools within the social network's software. What's really incredible about social networks is the wealth of personal private information gathered voluntarily from and consumers. On social networks, consumers will self-describe their interests and hobbies, their education and work background, their income levels, their geographical regions, where they shop, where they go, what they buy, and better yet - who their friends are. This is an extraordinary amount of useful marketing information that is available to anyone who wishes to advertise on the social network. Social Network advertising is extraordinarily easy and targeted, allowing a potential advertiser with even the most modest of budgets to reach tens of thousands of people virtually overnight for peanuts. The advertising platform built into social networks is, in fact, what pays for its existence.

Location-Based (Mobile) Social Networking
Location-Based Social Networking leverages Groundswell, Trust, Cults of Personality, Community, and Interconnectedness.

What You Need to Know

- Location-based marketing is the newest trend in social media and it leverages the power of smart phones.

- Applications are loaded on smart phones; the applications capture information about where the user is; this program provides more information about the merchant to the consumer and makes it easier for them to do business with the merchant.

- Further, users of these applications can win points, awards, discounts at participating merchants, promotional materials, or free merchandise – just by showing up.

- Location and award information is shared instantly with the user's social network giving an additional level of visibility and promotion to the merchant.

- Information collected through these applications can be aggregated and mined by merchants for business intelligence concerning consumer behavior.

Examples

- Foursquare

- Facebook Places

- QR-Codes

- Loopt

Description

Location-based marketing tools are software loaded onto consumer smart phones that allow a consumer to identify their location to their social network. That location could be a business or event, and simply for arriving and being there, the participant-consumer may be able to earn a reward in the form of discounts or free merchandize.

There are three sides to the location-based marketing strategy.

One side is the obvious benefit of a field reporter (the customer) actually announcing to their social network that they're at a store, event, promotion, sale, or something related to a business and its brand. That's good publicity. It could be made even better if they're *happy* – in other words, they just received some kind of incentive or reward for just being there – because they're likely to include some encouraging comments along with their update. Proliferation of the consumer's update could then encourage others to swing by to see all of the exciting things going on out there in your neck of the woods. On some location-based platforms, showing up somewhere actually earns them points and a dashboard of point progress is reflected back into their social community; people "win" by being the first, or, collecting more points than others, earning them titles and positions of prestige (example: becoming the Mayor of a Starbucks on Foursquare will earn you a free coffee).

Another side is the data collected from location-based marketing. Producers can use the information offered by these software providers (usually at a premium) to learn more about the behaviors, driving patterns, and interests of their customer base. If you think about it, a wealth of information can be obtained from the patterns consumers demonstrate as they "check-in" from one place to another – allowing marketers to see the time and distance travelled between locations, routine patterns of specific consumers as they obtain products and services every day, and how well consumers respond to certain promotions.

The last side is customer convenience and advertising. A QR-Code is a barcode that can be scanned-in by a cell phone and read by an online database. Depending on the function of the code, it could return additional information, advertising, or a survey to the end user on their cell phone about that company, brand, or products. It could also expedite the processing of information should the customer do business at that location. Personally, the QR-Code is a bit geeky: I just can't imagine lay-people not vested in the technology to start scanning barcodes at their own volition to answer a question that'd be easier answered by a human being, but granted, a lot of consumers are becoming trained to do this with other forms of barcode scanning software available to them on their smart phones.

The key to success in this kind of approach are incentives and timeliness. How can you reward your physical, onground visitor with material incentives for "playing" the game? Further, how can the immediacy and proximity of the consumer can be drawn upon to lure them into the store, event, or promotion.

Location-based marketing is new but it's a natural extension to social networks and builds off Mobility and Interconnectedness. It's also a huge data repository for marketers and helps complete the cycle of promotion and onground buy using social media; example: what is the amount of time that it takes to relay an idea in social media then have it acted upon by that party checking-in at the store? Then completing a purchase? How much did they spend when they arrived? Well, you could possibly understand that relationship using this technology. Look for location-based marketing to become ever-more present in the social media landscape. It may be a bit of an over-kill for the small business but enterprises will find the wealth of information an invaluable extension to their social media campaigns.

Follow-up Questions

1. Is there any cohesive strategy between your use of microblogging and social networking tools? Either in the name of your account, or, the messages that you use across either tool?

2. Have you standardized your use of tools to just a few? Are you spread too thin across the multitude of tools that're available to you?

3. Does your audience use the social networking or microblogging tool of your choice? Are they listening?

4. Does your Destination complement the content you're posting through social networks or microblogging platforms? Is the content related or unrelated? If so, how're you driving consumer interest to visit your Destination?

5. Are you aware of just how many leads and sales you already receive through social channels, or, from your company's website?

6. Are there clear calls-to-action on your Destination?

7. Is your website serving you? Is it a repository of curated, Long Tail information?

8. Are search engines tuned-in to your brand? How are your competitors using Search to be found more easily on the web?

9. How is Free being leveraged to your advantage? How is neglecting Free hurting your brand? What could you spare for Free on your Destination?

10. Are you using social networks to build Community, and are you listening to your audience? What's your listening strategy? How do you respond to concerns and complaints online?

References

1. December 13, 2010. Clendaniel, Morgan. Infographic: Is Anybody Reading Your Tweets? Found on the World Wide Web on December 29, 2010. URL: http://www.good.is/post/what-percent-of-people-check-twitter/

Part 4
What You Will Learn

- The importance of metrics in managing anything let alone a social media campaign

- The common forms of metrics – Traditional, Web Metrics, and Social Networking Metrics

- What Average Customer Lifetime Value (ACLV) is an how it can be used

- How we use metrics to dismiss the "everybody else is doing it" mentality

- How we use metrics to legitimize social media and to demonstrate real business results

Business and Measurement

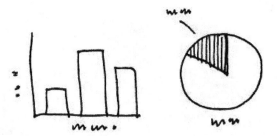

Often cited, it was Peter Drucker that said, "That which is not measured is not managed." Your intention to use social media must be met with a commitment to manage it. Measuring the performance of a social media effort is part of planning for its success.

Concerning the management of your business, there are a lot of measurements you already know and use. Your gross sales, payroll, taxes, and net profit; your balance sheet and cash flow; ratios that measure sales versus leads; the allowable costs you're willing to spend for attracting every dollar you earn. These are solid, material, and financial metrics that are easy for you to understand because you've been managing them since you've been running your business. Managing a social media campaign is no different ... except that the metrics we use don't directly involve, well, money.

The problem many have with social media is that the dollars spent in using it don't directly relate to anything useful. What does it mean if your company's Facebook page attracts 100 fans anyway? How does the acquisition of 100 fans and twenty "LIKES" this last week contribute to the bottom line? If you were to spend two hours blogging last week, how do you recoup the value of your time?

Directly, it doesn't, and you won't.

And now you're thinking, "If social media doesn't involve money and a returns aren't immediately obvious, heck, why am I reading this book?" As a business person, I'm confident you're not interested in social media strictly for the fun of it - you're expecting some kind of return – and you're right to ask that question. So I'm going to give it to you straight: there is no direct financial Return on Investment (ROI) from using social media; anyone who'd try to convince you otherwise is either disingenuous or confused.

That may sound a bit fishy coming from an author writing a book about social media for small business, but I simply want to be honest.

Instead, we tend to measure a different kind of ROI in social media - *Return on Influence* - whereas financial returns are an indirect consequence of influence. Influence can come in a variety of forms:

- Influence could be the powerful recommendation made by one of your customers to one of their friends on a social network;

- Influence could be the positive perception someone has when watching a video of your CEO;

- Influence could be a satisfied customer that uploaded a video to YouTube showing how to use your product, and it's seen by a just a couple hundred people;

- Influence might arise from your latest blog post where you contrasted the difference between your service and one of your competitors.

Anybody who has studied word-of-mouth marketing would attempt to convince you of the power of influence. It's influence of a friend that convinces us to buy a new product or try a new restaurant; the influence of a celebrity that assures how attractive we'll be if we wear their brand of jeans; the influence of a politician whose gained the trust of a neighbor; the influence of after sampling a new chef's cuisine. Hard-pressed as we are to quantify a specific financial return in any of these examples, you know as well as I that the value of such influence is that it may eventually translate into real dollars. Perhaps not immediately, but indirectly – after your influence compels a decision from a consumer. And thereafter the result is something measurable, tangible, and quantified.

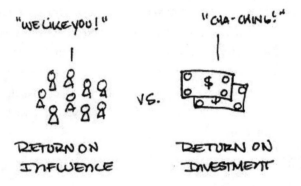

So it's not all gloom and bad news: there are indirect financial improvements eventually to be had but using social media isn't going to make you instant millions overnight, and a convenient ratio between dollars, time, and effort use doesn't exist. Not at all. Using social media strategically, however, will demand that you have a command over a variety of metrics – some you'll be used to and some will be new to you – but all of them attempt to look at ROI from social media as a measure of increased influence that will indirectly improve your traditional metrics.

Traditional Metrics

Now it may seem like I'm talking in circles, but the best way to measure the success of a social media campaign is to see its results reflected in your traditional metrics; those common measurements we were discussing earlier that you've been using all this time to run your business. They're the best because they're the most tangible – they're the results you're most familiar with and what you most desire as a business owner. Ultimately, see how your Return on Influence is working, you should have a very good baseline of the traditional measurements you're already used to.

Now, I can't emphasize this enough: you should have an established practice already for managing your business through measurements. A performance baseline will give you a picture of where your business is right now with a given metric – be it sales, profitability, error rates and scrap, market share. You should already know what those are, have a means of collecting data for measurement, have a regular frequency for review, and you should thoroughly understand how they're calculated. And if you don't, stop reading this book.

Yep. Right now. Seriously. Put it down. It's not going to do you any good. Social media is not going to make any difference to you if there's no way for you to measure its effects; if you've no clear understanding of where you are, how will you know if you've arrived?

Again, *"That which is not measured is not managed."*

Instead, you will want to reconsider investing in social media and instead concentrate on establishing root measurements of your business activity. You need to hone your management discipline. Go get that problem out of the way first and then come back to learning about social media. You'll thank me for it.

Web Metrics

Social media is a reflection of web technology and we can use web analytics to understand is performance and contribution to ROI (Return on Influence). In analyzing the results of our social media campaign, we can rely upon some common ways of measuring our performance in three categories: visitors, pages, and traffic.

- **Visitors.** On the web, we like to measure visitors in a lot of different ways. We like to measure the unique visitors they come to our website versus people who're simply returning. We like to be able to know about who the visitor is - perhaps their age and income demographics, where they're located, and what time of the day that they happened to visit. We may also be interested in information that describes how they're seeing our website; for example, consumers visiting our website on cell phones versus a regular computer, or what software they're using to interact with our site.

  We're always interested if our Destination is attracting more or less visitors from yesterday, the week before, the month before, are for the whole year. A spike in visitors may relate to a successful social media tactic; a drop in visitors may relate to an error, misjudgment, or tactical failure. Further, if we know more about our visitors then we can make the appropriate changes to our website to accommodate them. Fundamentally though, we're validating the effectiveness of our marketing efforts by gathering-up and aggregating data about visitors who come to our Destination.

- **Pages.** In the course of collecting data about visitors, we also tend to track other information concerning the pages found on our Destination. You're probably curious about which pages on your website gets the most traffic; which page search engines route visitors to; which page is usually the last one seen as a visitor exits your site? Tracking page information can also let us know when there's a malfunction on the page that could be preventing a spider from crawling the site, making it harder for search engines to index it. The more information that we have about our Destination, the more that we could be able to improve upon our site design and make it more useful as a marketing tool.

- **Traffic.** Where does a majority of traffic to your Destination come from? Which search engines are referring the most people more often to your site and why? Are other websites directly referring traffic to yours? What keywords did they use to find your content? Having some understanding of how visitors are connecting with your site is extremely valuable. In measuring the effectiveness of social media campaigns, we're particularly interested in the number of referrals passed by our social networks. We're also interested in how long visitors might stay on a page to read it, or, if they quickly "bounce" away; how long visitors stay on our site and what content they're most interested in.

Common Social Media Metrics

- **Network Reach and Density.** This is a fancy way of saying the number of followers that you might attract on Twitter, the number of connections you may acquire on Linked-In, or the number of fans who LIKE your Facebook page. Density - how many followers or fans or connections - answers one question, but what about 'where are they located?' Are they in your target markets or not? What would it take to acquire more audience from this neighborhood, town, city, state, or country? What would it take to acquire more audience from certain demographic segments like income, career, or educational background? And that's referred to as Reach. When you interact with your online community, the depth of your connections corresponds to a size of a potential audience. Successful social media campaigns are ones that both retains an audience and increases a brand's reach and density to meet strategic targets.

How to Use Facebook Insights' User Dashboard

- **Frequency of Updates.** The frequency of updates we provide on an online community can be both a positive and a negative for our campaign. On the negative side, if we talk too much and pander to our audience to extensively, they're likely to block our updates. They'll filter us out. Too many updates can give our audience an impression of being too spammy while too few updates could render our brand irrelevant – we're completely off their radar – and maybe we're missing opportunities to get our message out. Finding a balance between frequency and relevance desired by a brand's audience is part of the art and science of social media.

- **Number of Impressions.** When were participating on social networks, we're always intrigued to know how many times the our updates were shown to our audience. How many people actually saw what we said? Impressions are a count of times our update or advertisement was actually loaded onto the screen of user. Impressions aren't a direct count of our followers, though. Some users don't log in to a social network regularly and may miss seeing the update; some users will regularly filter our content and not see our update; our followers may have forwarded our content into their own social network. Impressions can increase exponentially if it's particularly relevant, important, or interesting, and that's the tall-tale indication of an idea that went 'viral' for you.

- **Number of Interactions.** If you're familiar with Facebook, then you're familiar with a 'thumbs-up' – a button that a user can click to indicate they approve or LIKE a status update that was posted. Similarly, an indicator of approval from fans on Twitter is a 're-tweet' where your update is shared with everybody else in another's social network. Exactly how many times does someone person present us with a thumbs up? How many times did someone stopped to comment on something that we posted? How many 're-tweets' did we get? These questions are directly related to developing an interested, listening, and engaged community on a social network. More interactions correlate to how interesting your content is and the relative attention span of your audience.

- **Ratio of Possibilities to Clicks.** Finally, as compared to all of the updates we provided our social network, what was the ratio of clicks – how many people acted by clicking on a hyperlink to our Destination? As a ratio of interactive to passive behavior, it gives us a glimpse into our ability to compel our audience to take action and do something. Like, click on a hyperlink that brings them to a video we placed on our Destination; to read a blog post we wrote; to participate in a survey; to sign-up for our electronic newsletter. A click is one of the more significant activities in social media because a click can drive traffic to your Destination, positively affecting the Web Metrics that we discussed earlier.

Web and Social Network Metrics are Tactical

Web and social media measurements gives us direct, observable, first-order effects on how well our social media campaigns are working. They allow us to see how our electronic community is responding to what we're saying, how effective our messages are, how relevant our ideas might be, and how important certain subjects are to our audience. Practically, I'd encourage you to think of them only as a tactical scorecard.

Sadly, there's no direct financial benefit from any of these activities as they're useful only in demonstrating that we're creating more visibility for our brand, traffic for our Destination, and influence among followers. Daily fluctuations in these measurements can be expected and effects like these aren't necessarily the catalyst for second-order impacts to Traditional Metrics that we so really desire. More visitors to our website doesn't necessary relate to more sales or revenue; more LIKES on Facebook won't necessary bring more foot traffic to our store. Strategically, we have to take a step back even further to measure broader behaviors and user activities that influence second-order financial effects found in Traditional Metrics.

Goals, Funnels, and Conversions

These are terms used quite extensively in explain search engine optimization (SEO) principles and they apply to social media as well. They're merely ways to view desirable, strategic effects from our social media campaign, and their relatively easy to understand.

- **Goals.** A goal is a desired managerial outcome in the real world. We're interested in using social media to improve the visibility of your business; to increase sales; to generate excitement about your brand; to make working with customers easier and more cost effective. A goal is a conservative, specific estimate of what you're looking for in your Traditional Metrics by engaging social media. Goals might be:

- Increase lead generation from the website by 5%

- Increase quarterly sales by 20%

- Collect another 100 subscriptions to your electronic newsletter

- Decrease call volume to our support desk by 10%

- Sell 80 more units of this widget

- Bring in 20 new clients to our salon every month

- Decrease call volume for routine questions to our staff by 5%

- Collect 3 positive customer testimonials a week

Notice that these are tangible, real-world things. A social media campaign must have a least one goal, i.e., why else would you be doing it in the first place? Do note that a Goal represents a specific, direct impact to your Traditional Metrics – measurements you should already know and be taking about your business – and it represents a real reason why you're engaging social media in the first place.

Now, here's where we get to question authority a bit. If the only reason why your company is embracing social media is because, well, "everybody else is doing it", then your social media campaign will obviously be fruitless; a *Return on Influence* will never show up in your Traditional Metrics. If that's the reason why you're engaging in social media, it'll eventually become necessary to reshape that expectation. Sure, everyone is using social media, but why? Why is your company using social media? Those who can answer that question are light-years ahead of the competition. They have purpose and their social media strategy has real-world meaning.

That said, it's not too uncommon to reflect Goals in terms of first-order effects. "Increase the number of unique visitors to our Destination by 20%", or, "Increase the number of Twitter followers by 200", or, "Obtain five likes per week on Facebook", or, "Improve our click a ratio by 5%". These Goals will improve Influence and may be entirely valid to you as a manager of a social media campaign.

Regardless if you're looking at first or second-order effects, Goals are managerial outcomes that attempt to explain what the campaign is supposed to do in a meaningful way. Specificity is important and baselines are important; like I was mentioning earlier, second-order effects won't be realized unless you've already a process for capturing that data. You have to know where you are and where you intend to go for any social media campaign to be successful.

- **Funnels.** Influence will drive more traffic to your Destination and there are certain areas on our website that are more important than others. Our product catalog, for instance, or, a contact us form, or, a newsletter subscription form, an online coupon, our sales lead generation form, a description of a book we wrote, or a white paper we've published. If more visitors land on such content, it may denote that our Influence to bring them to these locations is improving. Visitors landing on these pages – or clicking on this content – are very close to taking action: to doing something that'd have a first-order effect. Therefore, the interactions between visitors and such content on our Destination directly relates to our Goal. We call these things Funnels.

  Landing on a Funnel doesn't necessarily translate into a 'buy' behavior but the consumer is very close to making that decision. Funnels are events and activities on our Destination that indicate our audience is listening, responding, and is prepared to take action. More frequent hits against the Funnel absolutely demonstrates that our Influence is working – after all, our efforts brought them to this point – and now we're left to seal the deal; to perform a Conversion.

- **Conversions.** A Conversion is a measurement of a desired action that achieves a Goal. That action may be the submission of one e-mail address to receive your electronic newsletter; the download of a coupon; a visitor who walks into your storefront with a promo-code they found online; another sale of a widget. That's a success!

Conversions can be measured in sales and dollars; people who commit to following you on social networks; sales; leads; telephone calls; the number of people who respond and interact with you on social networks; the number of times a product brochure is downloaded; if somebody contacts you across the web or from visiting your destination. There are many ways to measure a Conversion but no matter how we do it, conversion should measure an action that contributes to your Goal. Conversions are, in fact, the Holy Grail in any social media campaign: more Conversions equal your meeting the Goal.

Average Customer Lifetime Value (ACLV)

I like to present this calculation in the classroom because it helps bring more financial incentive to social media, and I find that business leaders identify more with the concept of money than first-order benefits from Influence.

Average Customer Lifetime Value (ACLV) this is the average gross amount of revenue that one customer will bring your company in the lifetime of service to them.

Here's an example: if you're a professional photographer and a typical customer will spend an average of $160 per session and $240 in prints, and most customers will engage your services for an average of three sessions, then that's an ACLV of $1,200. Each client will gross you an average of $1,200.

Having understood that number, what's the amount of money that you're prepared to spend to acquire a customer? That's called an Allowable Cost per Sale (ACS). If you think you're willing to spend maybe 10% of your ACLV to acquire a customer, then you're saying you're willing to spend – in this case – up to $120 per customer.

Now let's say that you set up a Facebook page for your business. After a while, you get some people to follow you, inquire about your company, and read the content found on your Destination. After a few months, you build Influence and Trust, and your metrics reveal that a Facebook Conversion happens in about 1 of every 10 followers; that's a Conversion Rate. Meanwhile, setting up and using Facebook is free but your time is valuable so let's say you price your hourly rate at $45 and you spend one hour a week on status updates and uploading new pictures and content. In one week, you attract an average of 3 new followers. Okay, here's the fun math:

- New Facebook Followers Annually: 156

- Conversion Rate (CR): 15

- CR x ACLV: $18,000

- Less Annual Time Investment: $2,340

- Net Average Lifetime Revenue: $15,660

- Allowable Cost Per Sale (ACS) Benchmark: ($120 x 15) = $1,800

- ACS Actual: ($2,340/15 = $156)

- Straight ROI: ~768%

In this example, we spent a little more on Allowable Costs than we'd like and maybe we'd adjust our Allowable Cost per Sale, or, work on ways to reduce our cost/time on Facebook to control your costs. Still, not a bad return on your social media marketing effort, and you can see where it benefits to do more: the average return on your time spent is so small. What other form of marketing can you think about a 768% straight ROI? And those are frankly conservative estimates for a relatively small social media campaign effort.

Conclusion

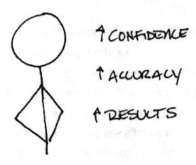

The art of managing social media is like any other form of management and it requires you to understand metrics, baselines, and variances. Establishing a discipline of managing metrics will allow you to manage social media campaigns effectively and will allow you to talk intelligently about its benefits. The inverse of this is to have no measurements, no understanding of benefits or conversions, and is simply presume that all is well and that social media is paying off for you. You're only doing it because "everybody else is". I don't know about you but assumptions like these don't help me sleep better and they certainly don't help me execute.

Follow-up Questions

1. How does your company measure Traditional Metrics? What are they? Are they frequently used, gathered, interpreted, and acted-upon? Who manages them? Who sees them? How important are those Traditional Metrics to management's decision-making?

2. What tools are you using to measure first-order effects? An example that I've used is Google Analytics. Do you or your social media campaign managers have the necessary technical training to use those tools?

3. What are the Goals behind using social media at your firm? What does the boss want? What do you want? Get specific: how will your Goals be measured from first-order effects? What pages on your Destination are candidate Funnels, and what events comprise of a Conversion? How will first-order effects translate into second-order effects on your Traditional Metrics?

4. If you've hired a consultant or external social media manager, how are you holding them accountable? Which first-order effects or second-order effects will

their engagement be measured by? How can you encourage better performance through incentives?

5. How will greater influence translate into second-order effects in your business?

6. Are there minimum-levels of first-order effects that you'd like to consider? Are there targets that you feel your Destination should be constantly achieving?

7. How do you currently measure and track your sales leads? How can social media be fit into that process as a separate channel?

8. Is there a budgetary process for advertising and promotion in your company? How should social media fit into that process?

9. Given the growth of social media and the rapidly-changing landscape, what sources of information are you going to follow to learn more about measuring social media and making it more meaningful to your business?

10. How could measurements prove a political argument inside of your company regarding the role and value of social media? What would be sufficient evidence to convince your naysayers? How could that data be collected, gathered, and presented?

References

Part 5

What You Will Learn

- Why it's valuable to plan and assign roles and responsibilities to tasks

- The importance of storytellers

- How social media can be executed in cycles to address multiple aspects of a small business

- How social media campaigns establish a paper trail for demonstrating material success

- How plans are used as political instruments to garner confidence and positively impact opinion

Social Media Campaign Planning

B 8 Strategic Values from Technology Investments

Having covered a suitable degree of essential concepts, now let's discuss how we can put some of these ideas into action. Preparing a social media campaign isn't difficult but there needs to be – above all – a plan: a documented, thoughtful strategy that describes a process to use social media, establishes accountability, and clarifies your Goals.

A plan implies that there's some strategic-thinking behind your use of social media, that you're not launching into it on a wing and a prayer. Too often in my practice have I seen companies embrace social media without fully understanding its purpose, benefits, metrics, or effects, whereas the end result is always predictable: chaos, disappointment, and missed expectations.

Your social media campaign plan will address:

- **Who's In Charge.** Planning should be delegated to an individual with accountability for the strategy. Should that be a senior manager, the CEO, a dedicated position or a consultant, or the president of the small business -

somebody needs to be held accountable for executing the plan. Without accountability, it's very unlikely that any material, second-order impact can be made with a social media campaign.

- **Executive Commitment.** An accountable party must have some kind of fiscal authority. Most of the cost necessary to execute a social media campaign will come inexpensively, but at the consequence of time and labor that could be doing something else. It'd really be inappropriate to hand somebody the reins of a project without appropriate resources or authority needed to complete it. Even if it's the most modest of budgets, there should be some dollars reserved for achieving your marketing goals.

- **Roles and Responsibility.** Hopefully you'll select people who're familiar with social media. If not, perhaps somebody from marketing with direct mail or word-of-mouth advertising experience. Barring professional marketing experience, maybe someone who is familiar with social networks and not intimidated by a computer? And beyond that, if there are no other qualified candidate, perhaps you should think of a consulting engagement or recruiting for full-time position? Hand the challenges of running a social media campaign to someone who's either disinterested or unfamiliar with the territory is a recipe for disaster.

- **Appropriate Skills.** The parties you select to participate on the campaign should be pretty good at writing copy and it'd be even better if this person is good at public speaking, visual graphic design, video or audio media, web technology, and honestly: it doesn't hurt to see a touch of the eccentric in this person. They need to be a great communicator both on and off the screen and present an interesting, affable personality. Throwing a dull person at a project like this who doesn't speak well, who doesn't have the skill-set to manage the medium, who doesn't get social marketing, and who is more of an introvert, is going to be highly problematic for you.

Words of Advice and Caution

- **Do not delegate this project to your web developer.** Your web developer is good at managing and creating your Destination and can help implement the tools necessary to execute the campaign. That said, your developer is probably very bad at understanding your business model, your products, and your customers. That means you need somebody from the inside.

- **Do not delegate this project to an operations manager.** This individual already has a realm of responsibilities that comply with your Traditional Metrics. They already have enough "real-world" things to do. They're not likely to be very keen on inheriting new obligations and responsibilities that may seem outside of the realm of their usual business (like preparing videos, blog content, or facilitating online discussions). Social media will only frustrate them.

- **Do not causally delegate this project to an intern, a family member, or computer geek you know.** In the best of circumstances, this is going to be somebody close to your internal processes, or, somebody who can learn about those processes very quickly and speak well about them. Someone who is vested in the company's success.

- **Do not be too hasty.** The pendulum of Influence can swing in both directions – positively and negatively. Remember that this is your business and a promotion activity. Choose wisely and act responsibly.

- **Do intend to monitor the progress of this project.** Simply because it's delegated for execution doesn't excuse your involvement as a senior executive or owner. You may even want to be regularly involved with the campaign.

- **Do legitimize authority and responsibility.** If you're looking for the full-time position, I'd recommend one of two titles: Community Manager or Social Marketing Manager. The first implies that social media is being used to be able to create and Foster a sense of community centered around the brand. The second is more traditional and implies that there's a marketing purpose behind using social media and that the title is only fitting. Within organizations, political legitimacy is created through titles. Take this opportunity to legitimize the social media process and bring meaning to the work.

Beginning Elements

Before embarking in any campaign, you must have a few critical technical elements in place, and now we can start using the *big-boy* vocabulary we've learned thus far:

- You must have a Destination.

- Your Destination should have a Blog. Blogging should begin right away.

- Your Destination should have a clear Call-to-Action. Promotions, coupons, white-papers, or other content should be readily prepared for public consumption.

- You company must have a social networking account. I'd recommend Facebook.

- Your brand should set up a Page on Facebook. That will give you access to Facebook's internal social metric system called Insights.

- Your social networking Page should be integrated with your Destination. Talk to your web developer.

- You should have a microblogging account in the name of your business or brand. I'd recommend Twitter.

- Your microblogging account should be integrated with your destination. Again, talk to your web developer. Integrating Twitter and Facebook into your Destination is relatively common. Integration helps lead visitors to your social media presence online.

- Your Destination should be SEO-optimized to improve Search. Your web developer likely offers an SEO service.

- Your Destination should be using Google Analytics to capture first-order effects. Your web developer can install the technical prerequisites to enable Analytics.

You should not begin a social media campaign until these basic elements are in place. The reasons should be obvious but let's do a cursory review to explain why.

- **Our Destination is our web property.** If you're generating more Influence, you need to direct consumers to a specific place such as a web site with content. If your Destination is incomplete or under repair, you're only hurting the first-impression opinion consumers have of your product are service. Therefore, your destination should be finished and ready for public consumption.

- **Our Destination Calls-to-Action.** When visitors arrive, you want a clear and obvious path for doing something, be it calling your company, be it subscribing for a newsletter, be it downloading a white paper, scheduling appointment, or buying something. Without the call to action, driving traffic to your destination will be less than effective.

- **Our Destination relates ideas back to our brand.** We've spoken at-length on how blogs are used to generate content and convince search engines of your authority in specific areas. Your blog associates those ideas with your destination. Your blog should be up and running, adding new content, for least a month before you begin the social media campaign. Establish a regular discipline. Don't allow new potential customers to arrive in your web site and find an empty or partially written blog. They won't think highly of it.

- **Our Destination is easily found and seen online.** Also, if we're directing search engine spiders back to your Destination, we want them to be able to easily find and index content. It should be easy for spiders to crawl your website and report back upon what they found. Broken links, missing information, or failures in the crawl should be avoided.

- **Social Networking is our Channel.** Social networks and microblogging platforms will help distribute our content and will help pull visitors back to our Destination. These accounts become the mouthpiece for your organization and will help you build community. They will come to represent you and your "channel" to a potentially-vast audience.

- **We must measure to be effective and successful.** And finally, we have to be tactically and strategically prepared to measure results. First-order and second-order effects; Goals, Funnels, and Conversions. You should have analytics capabilities online and understand how to use those tools before you get started.

Beginning Strategies

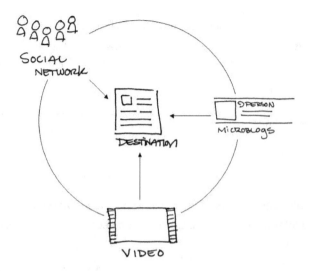

In the realm of consultants, there are plenty of ideas surrounding how social media should be implemented. Some are elaborate and expensive; others are almost entirely too simplistic. In my opinion, starting with the basics isn't a bad approach, particularly if you're new to social media. Any small business can start out with four basic strategies to leverage social media, and they are referred to as Pull, Portal, Community, and Promotion.

The Pull Strategy. Most social media campaigns exercise a content Pull Strategy – also known as a "Donut Marketing Strategy". It relies upon you to create content that elaborates on your core competencies. When new content is added to your Destination, your audience is encouraged (or pulled) to visit your website to read, view, or watch it; when new content is added elsewhere on the web, it points back to your Destination.

Benefits

- The backwards-facing links generated by this strategy improve Search and web visibility because search engines believe your website to be an authority in its niche.

- When new content is added to your Destination your Long Tail grows; that ultimately relates more keywords, concepts, and ideas back to your brand.

- The Pull Strategy generates more traffic to your Destination. First-order effects will be habitually bursty: when new content is posted, traffic will spike, and thereafter return to normal levels, then spike again when new content is posted.

 micklerr Russell Mickler
Creative Destruction in the New Economy
http://reinventwork.com/creative-destruction-in-the-new-economy/
5 Jan

- Pull Strategies can be directed towards Funnels where consumers encounter a call-to-action, Convert, and second-order effects can be realized.

Implementation Examples

- Once a new blog post is generated at your Destination, a microblog alerts your audience to come read it.

- Once a new blog post is generated at your Destination, a mass-email is released along with the hyperlink encouraging your audience to read it.

- Once a new release of your newsletter has been uploaded, a microblog alerts your audience to come download it.

- Once new video or pictures have been uploaded, a microblog alerts your audience to come see it.

- A weekly podcast or vidcast can recap the post and elaborate upon it, again bringing your audiences' attention back to your content, your expertise, and your Destination.

- When any new content is published, it can be shared with a social network to draw your Community back to your Destination.

When any new content is published, you can use Tagging an Social Bookmarks to help its online visibility.

Big Picture Ideas About This Strategy

- The content you create and distribute should educate rather than sell. Avoid looking spammy to your audience. Instead, focus on providing real value with each update.

- Look at new content as your Destination's *pulse*. It allows your brand to look dynamic and alive to both consumers and search engines. If you're not posting new content and pulling visitors back to read it, your brand is stoic, silent, and placid – boring. Search engines won't rank your website well and you're not attracting visitors through social media.

- Keep a regular schedule for providing updates. Practically, two or three times a week is sufficient although many social media experts would tell you several times daily is desirable. Myself, I feel that approach could run the risk of getting your brand filtered by consumers. Just concentrate on quality, valuable content offered at regular intervals inside of a week.

The Portal Strategy. Over time, your Destination can be developed into a Long Tail repository of information, downloads, white papers, FAQ's, articles, blog posts, press releases, video, presentations – a wealth of information in your niche. Content added to your Destination can reduce costs associated with reproduction and distribution to clients and shareholders. Ideas expressed in this media are indexed by spiders and related back to your brand and establish your Destination as an authority on these issues to search engines. Older content will drive a reliable stream of traffic to your website to create a regular baseline of activity against more bursty traffic generated by content Pull.

Benefits

- More content allows your Destination to become an authority on a niche.

- Curated content extends self-service opportunities to customers, or illustrates your company's solutions to common sales questions, creating desirable second-order effects.

- Content added to the curated Destination improves authoritative visibility and search engine rankings.

- Over time, other websites, social bookmarking sites, and social networks will link to your content creating more backwards-facing links, improving search engine rankings.

- More content establishes expertise in a certain subject matter, extending value to consumers looking for such information.

- Content can be used to self-service education and information for customers.

Implementation Examples

- A doctor can load many pieces of generic information that they'd normally distribute to their clients by hand to their website. That automates distribution and makes it easier for the patient to work with the doctor. And as a second-order effect, it eliminates the costs for reproduction and distribution.

- A company can provide short video tutorials on how to use their products, or, how a business process is performed in the field, and deters repetitive phone calls – lowering costs as a second-order effect.

- Forms, manuals, and instructions can be loaded online, eliminating the cost for reproduction and distribution – a second-order effect.

- Presentations, tutorials, customer and product testimonials can be loaded to help educate and win the consumer's confidence. That could lead to more Conversions and increase sales as a second-order effect.

- Pictures of recent happy customers, successful product launches, community events, any job well-done, your company's annual picnic or sales event – almost like an electronic photo album - can help generate buzz and personify your brand.

Big-Picture Ideas About this Strategy

How Can I Re-Engineer a Business Process?

- What is almost everything you created became available online? Available to anyone who needed it – either publicly or securely – could be directed to a single portal: your Destination?

- Any document or form that is faxed, emailed, or otherwise given to somebody anywhere should be available exclusively online, aiding in cost-containment and labor-reduction.

- What if your website became a portal for calendaring and scheduling, payment settlements, internal collaboration and document sharing, or consumer interaction? Eliminating duplicative software in-house?

- If the Destination became a single point of capability for your company, your business could operate anywhere – on any device - without relying upon internal software or server equipment.

- How can your Destination become a scaleable self-service tool that extends services and value to a growing customer base without incurring additional costs to you?

- How can content relay both expertise and emotion to compel visitors to act?

The Community Strategy. Social networks can be leveraged to provide feedback – to be listened to. When content is added to your Destination, a question might be raised on your social network to ask a Community for their opinion on the issue, giving you an opportunity to facilitate a discussion, solicit feedback, or to just encourage a response. Entire themes of ideas could be facilitated through interrogative questions, or through polling or surveys, that indirectly relates to the problems posed by your content. Community Strategy allows you to tap into the Groundswell surrounding your product and service.

Benefits

- Listening. The customer gets to express their opinions directly to you like a comment card. That information can be used to transform business processes.

 Renay Shanel 🔖 Why are people complaining and talking of how horrid the Trenta is? If you don't like it, don't order it. I mean obviously you are not a loyal Starbucks drinker if you dislike this. Embrace that it's a smile in a cup, they are listening to their customers needs. I am excited with this idea and congratulate Starbucks on their new launch #Starbucks Gold Member4life ♥
13 hours ago · View Post

- Higher-level interaction. Instead of compelling your audience to click for new content, you're asking for their opinion. This is more cognitive in nature.

- Further, your questions may also solicit social media content (pictures, video, blog posts) from your Community.

- Can be combined with a Pull Strategy to gain similar benefits.

- Your Community may forward your ideas into their own extended social network. This activity extends the Reach of your brand and builds loyalty.

Implementation Examples

- A new blog post available at your Destination talks about a certain subject. Re-phrase that subject into an opinion question for your Community.

- Give your own opinion on a news item that concerns your city or industry. Pick a topic that a majority of your audience could relate to, and give a short, tasteful opinion about it. That may encourage others to share their opinion with you.

- Create a poll on a product or service issue.

- Admit to a failure your business recently had to endure. Ask for your Community's opinion on how you might make improvements.

- Showcase a new business success with pictures, video, testimonials, or a case study.

- Conduct an interview with a prominent member of your company, employee, or board of directors using the social network, or, with video.

- Admit that you were wrong. Go ahead, it's cathartic. If you or your staff mistreated somebody or handled an incident poorly, post it to your Community and – to those affected by the incident – offer an incentive for them to return.

- Say something silly or upload a quirky picture. Something tasteful yet a tiny bit eccentric, and hopefully it's a little funny. Doing so helps humanize your brand.

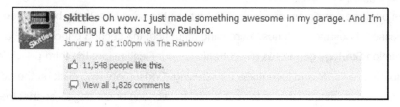

Skittles Oh wow. I just made something awesome in my garage. And I'm sending it out to one lucky Rainbro.
January 10 at 1:00pm via The Rainbow

👍 11,548 people like this.

💬 View all 1,826 comments

Big Picture Ideas About This Strategy

- Listen and never sell. Now is the time to talk *with* your Community and not *at* your Community. Engage them.

- This is hard for most small business owners to grasp but a Community Strategy is all about them: your Community.

- Ask questions, solicit feedback, listen to what they have to say – positive or negative – and always respond politely.

- Ask for meaningful opinions. Get people passionate about what you're discussing and that will help produce a meaningful response. If you ask closed (yes/no) questions, or fail to ask any relevant question at all, your Community will be unlikely to respond with more than a "thumbs-up".

- Community is a reputation-building exercise that accentuates Trust. Over the long term, consider how you're convincing your Community to trust you, your opinions, and your expertise. Be transparent and open, polite and courteous.

- Be authentic. Skip the corporate jargon. Consumers will do business with *you* – because they like and trust *you*. Online Communities can see right through *fake*.

The Promotion Strategy. Social networks offer an opportunity for direct marketing. Facebook, for example, has a very simple yet elegant means of reaching a very targeted audience. Online advertising through social networks is a great way to build more Influence, generate more followers or fans, or disseminate important, timely information inexpensively. The Promotion Strategy relies upon tailoring ads, coupons, and promotions released to your social network Community and microblogging audience, and may leverage location-based social marketing. It relies on three principles: one is visibility, where the ad is constantly being seen an impressed thousands of times, increasing Influence; the second principle is that the Promotion Strategy generates direct traffic to your Destination; the third principle are to offer rewards and incentives for listening. Consumers who click on the ad are brought to our destination - or to your social networking home page - so that they can explore more of what the ad was telling them. This campaign strategy is cost-effective because you only pay for the click: your brand, logo, tagline, or ideas may

be subconsciously seen tens of thousands of times by a specific market segment at
no additional cost to you. You only pay for what generates traffic to your
Destination.

Benefits

- Online advertising is an inexpensive means of reaching a very targeted
  audience and attracting them to your Funnels.

- Incentives offered through promotions extend incentives for consumers to
  pay attention to your updates and new content.

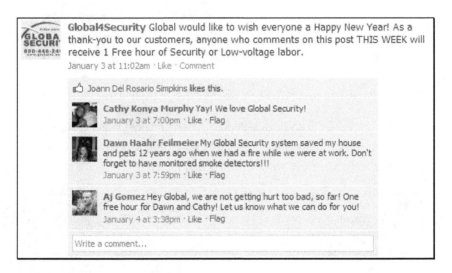

- Location-based incentives can leverage social media to drive foot-traffic to
  local storefronts, and can cross-promote your business into their social
  network.

- Video, pictures, and a stream of updates from an event will pique interest
  and keep visitors returning to your Destination for the latest news.

- Promotion Strategy can harness the immediacy of this medium by
  drawing-in physical customers to the actual location of your business –
  now.

Implementation Examples

- Use Facebook as a pay-per-click advertising platform. Create targeted ads that focus on one simple aspect of your business, pointed to a Funnel on your Destination. Your message and logo will be impressed tens of thousands of times and you'll only pay for the click – the traffic it provides to your website.

- Offer promotion codes, discounts, and coupons across your social network.

- Microblog "instant" promotions that are only available right now, or, within the hour. Provide incentives to always be listening.

- If you're a baker a new muffins just came out of the oven, microblog them with a picture. Everybody loves hot muffins. They may actually purchase them, too, if they know they're fresh and available now.

- Mass-email distribution for newsletters and promotions.

- If you're traveling and available for a lunch or dinner in the area, share it. Never miss an opportunity to engage in on-ground networking with customers and peers, or see friends and family.

 micklerr Russell Mickler
Fri Jan 21, 4pm-6pm, I'll be at the Portland Beer & Blog held at the GreenDragon in PDX, Oregon http://portland.beerandblog.com/
12 Jan

- Leverage Google Places to create a reference back to your local business.

- Encourage your social network Community to "check-in" with a Location-Based application or QR-Code the next time they're at your retail storefront.

- Provide incentives/discounts for "check-ins".

- Promote everything you can with video. A short, 30-second video explaining an event, sale, or promotion, shared throughout your social network and embedded on your Destination is very desirable.

- If you're promoting an event, use microblogging, social networks, and location-based social media to give quarter-hour updates about what's going on. Maybe even video. This will generate buzz and hype over the event, and keep people interested in its content.

> **La Bottega in Vancouver, WA** Tuesday for dinner at La Bottega! bottles of wine under $50 will be half price between 5 & 9 PM, 750ml bottles only. Saucy, cheesy, full of flavor sausage & mushroom lasagna. Smooth & creamy mushroom soup. Tasty pastrami & provolone sandwich with dijon, mayonnaise, basil, onion, sun dried tomato, & spinach on sourdough! All so delicious!
> about an hour ago

- Use a Pull Strategy in conjunction with a Promotion Strategy. Pull visitors into a Funnel found on your Destination to answer a small questionnaire or survey. After completing the survey, the visitor may have access to an e-book, a coupon, or a free product/service.

- Offer incentives for sharing and for referrals. Make it really easy to share your store, product, or contact information.

Big Picture Ideas About This Strategy

- *Incentives for membership* is really what this strategy is all about. Some social media statistics show that one of the largest reasons consumers follow brands on social networks are to receive discounts and promotions.

- What can you offer to your "club" of followers that your competitors can't?

- However, it's not always about the money. The largest reason consumers follow brands on social networks are to show their support behind a product or individual. Some also believe following the brand is fun!

> **Applebee's** For those 21 or older...Margarita: salted or unsalted?
> January 12 at 12:16pm
>
> 👍 414 people like this.
>
> 💬 View all 985 comments

- The Promotion Strategy takes the immediacy of the medium and the interconnectedness provided by social networking to offer incentives for visiting physical locations. Adoption projections concerning the use of location-based marketing and social coupons are skyrocketing; the success of giants like Groupon and Foursquare only illustrate its potential. Both will become a significant component to social media strategy over the next eighteen months.

Create a Social Media Campaign Plan

Document Template: A Social Media Campaign Planner for Small Business

Planning for a social media campaign is very much like planning for any other kind of marketing campaign. We first one to identify some practical elements about the company and its goals surrounding this marketing effort. Right off the bat, the elements that we'd want to first identify describe the company and the campaign's purpose.

- Company name

- Company city and state

- Duration of campaign (days)

- Business goals

- Accountability

Each of these elements are fairly self explanatory but let's step through them anyway.

First we're trying to identify the **company** and its **geographic location** that the campaign will be used for. We may even be attempting to promote a specific regional office within the campaign instead of a corporate presence, and that'd have some bearing on our message. Geography, meanwhile, has some influence the use of tools we'd use in the promotion, how we will influence consumer behavior, and the Reach and Depth we're looking for from the social network. It's an anchoring-point for us to remember who we're trying to promote within the scope of the campaign.

The **duration** of campaign is measured in days - I would recommend a duration no longer than 15 days. And why 15 days? Well, in "Internet Time", things move very quickly, as does the attention span of an audience. Attention is fleeting on the web – if you don't believe me, just watch how many times you'll see cat videos from your own social network feed. It's easy to get distracted on the web. In my opinion, planning on 15 day campaign rotations gives you a manageable, two-campaigns-a-month approach to implementing social media. It's more than enough to get started and not so infrequent as to lose the attention of your audience.

Business goals may be fairly consistent for each campaign and might include such broad statements as: increase brand awareness, improve profitability, attract more customers, reinforce brand, generate sales leads and so on. These are a real-world purpose that will have tangible meaning and benefit to the business. Don't have more than three; it's better just to have one. Think clearly about why you're launching this campaign and what its purpose is for. Remember that you'll have ample opportunity later in future campaigns to address other business goals.

Accountability directly speaks to the person who will be in charge for executing the campaign. If you're the business owner, this may be your title, or, the title of the individual delegated the authority and responsibility to execute. It is purely identifying a party who'll be responsible for implementing the strategy and coordinating the diverse amount of resources to make it successful.

Goals

As we discussed earlier in Part Four, Goals are reflection of management's intent and management's desired outcomes for running the social media campaign. It's perfectly acceptable to have one Goal; you should have no more than three goals. One campaign cannot and will not do everything. Instead, the campaign is niched to do one outcome or maybe two outcomes well. Be realistic in what you hope to accomplish.

Destination Assessment

In order for you to carry out your goals and to be able to execute the campaign, certain things must exist on your Destination and may actually be required for you to carry out the campaign. You should critically assess your Destination to see whether or not it contains - or requires - any of the following elements to make the campaign work:

- An About Section

- Executive Biographies

- Product and Service Descriptions

- A Shopping Cart or Order Processing Solution

- A Contact Us Section

- A Self-Service Section

- News and Current Events in Your Industry or for Your Company

- Articles, FAQ's, or White Papers

- Aggregation or Feeds

- Online Request for Service or Feedback

- A Blog

- Video

- Social Media Badges/Integration

- Social Bookmarking and Tagging Tools

Most of these things you may already have on your Destination; others you may be lacking. It may not be that important if they're missing - perhaps it could be a future goal - but one of these elements is going to be a Funnel for this campaign.

You may be driving people and traffic to your executive biographies; you may be driving them to contact you using the website; you may want them to buy something using your shopping cart; you may have them read your blog; you may want them to watch your video; you may want them to read a white paper. What's your Call-to-Action?

Be honest with this assessment. You're looking for any disconnects that would prevent the strategy from working. What you're attempting to do here is critique your Destination before you launch the campaign to make sure it has the components necessary to execute. Your answers to this assessment will also give you an indication of what sections on your Destination should be monitored to witness Funnel effects.

Products and Services

It's important to think about the different kinds of products and services that you'll be promoting within the scope of this campaign. Not every campaign can address the wide range of services that you might offer. No marketing campaign should ever attempt to convey too many ideas. Alternatively, consider the campaign a tightly-focused effort to explain just one value, service, or product, in one market, to a specific consumer demographic. Think about that because it'll help craft the messages you'll need to promote them. At best, think about one product or one service that will be promoted within the scope of this campaign; at worst, consider two or three, but no more.

Competitive Survey

You can learn quite a bit by studying your competitors. Take a look at your market competitors and how they're using their Destination to market similar products and services to a similar demographic. Evaluate the way that they're using their Destination and social networks-blogging, video, communities, forms, feeds and podcasts, and microblogging. What are they doing right? What are they doing wrong? Ask yourself these questions:

- Who is your competitors audience and stakeholders?

- How are your competitors using social media to build Trust with their stakeholders?

- Who are your competitor storytellers? Are they line level employees, professional markers, or the CEO?

- How is your competitor using social media to promote their expertise and experience?

- How are your competitors responding to their Community? Are they actually ignoring the Community or fostering it, developing it?

- How are your competitors not using social media effectively? What would they need to change?

Answering any one of these questions will give you a competitive advantage because you're learning from their experience. It also gives you a way to maybe improve your approach and to differentiate yourself from your competitor. Seriously, watch your competitors: you might be surprised at how adept – or inept – they are with their own social media strategy. This could give you some very important insights about their management style, their priorities, their spending on web-based advertising, and what they think social media can be used for.

Branding

Consider your company's brand or image. How will the social marketing campaign attempt to reinforce or reposition that image?

In the campaign plan, try to describe your brand's image as it currently exists today. What are some clear ideas that your brand and products convey? Then, think about how the social media campaign affects that image. If it won't reposition the image, then it's reinforcing what your brand is already all about. Now, how will the social media campaign do that? How can your brand get closer and develop more trust with the target consumer? How can it reinforce what you're already about, or, slightly change public perception?

Now you have an opportunity to think about what your brand could *say* if it had a voice. What you want your product to say? What would you want your company to say? Social media is the voice of your business. You must clearly think about what this campaign is going to attempt to do to your brand when you give it that voice.

Storytellers

Good marketing is all about telling a small story.

Whether or not we're telling a story through images, through video, or through narrative, we're talking to consumers in a metaphor. Stories are the easiest way that people can retain and remember ideas.

Your storytellers are those that you've charged to use social media to relate their story and to help execute your social media strategy. Your storytellers maybe people from within the organization, maybe your social media manager, your senior officer in charge of operations, volunteers, patrons, it could even be a board member or your company's president. Sometime storytellers are even your customers – and those storytellers are really the best – because is there testimonials that ensure other consumers to trust you.

Think about your storytellers now. Once you've identified storytellers, you might wanna think about how they're going to convey their message. Some storytellers may do much better using video than the written word; testimonials are fantastic on video; others may offer to donate their time blogging. Within the scope of a single campaign, there should be no more than three and it is certainly fine to just have one. Make sure they're a good fit for the campaign. And you'll want to rotate-in new storytellers for new campaigns to keep your message and image fresh online.

Then relate what core competencies and intellectual property, or products and services, that would be the best fit for your storyteller. The storyteller should be familiar with what you do, what you offer, and what experiences they've had with you in the past. Line these up and assign responsibilities. You're then creating a sense of accountability and ownership to be able to help execute the strategy.

Campaign Message and Feedback

Overall, what is the message that you're trying to get across? Does the message somehow correlate with the ideas about your brand? What is the moral of the story you're trying to convey? How does the story leverage or relate to your products and services, or to what you're really good at – your intellectual property and core competencies?

You should identify key ideas, keywords, and phrases that could all be used to help promote this campaign. This is a creative exercise - you're trying to express how your products or services extend value to every customer in a way that fits the campaign. Will your story be soft, quiet, or gentle? Will your story be humorous and outrageous? Will your story be serious and important? Will your story inspire or offend? All of these approaches are tactics in crafting your marketing message. And none of this is complicated. Here's a couple of ideas to think about:

- Describe the story for your campaign

- How does the story leverage your storytellers, your intellectual property, or your core competency?

- What is your listening strategy? How you collect feedback and interact with your customer?

- What are some potential ideas, keywords, and phrases that you wish to emphasize?

Having an answer to these questions will help you manage the campaign, create content, post relevant status updates, engage your audience, and set an overall theme. Play with this. Offer your customer variability throughout campaigns - nobody wants to hear the same story, told over and over again, in the same way, by the same people; that makes for very dull brand. Tell new stories, tell exciting stories, tell stories that they're going to remember!

Landing Page Assessment

As a part of evaluating your Destination, it's important to look at some SEO characteristics of your Funnels. Here are some common and important ideas. If some of this is a little obtuse, you may want to talk to your web developer to make sure these ideas are being carried out.

- **Page Title.** The title of your Funnel should describe your product, market, or target consumer in less than 80 characters, which has a lot to do with the way spiders understand your web page and categorize it. Your Funnel page's title should fit what you're trying to accomplish with the campaign.

- **Page Description.** The description of your Funnel should be expressed in 160 characters or less. Just like the title, descriptions provide a bit more text to help explain what your web pages about. You should try to describe your target market, consumer, or your product in the description.

- **Page Content.** Your Funnel should contain the keywords, phrases, and ideas you identified earlier in under 300 words of narrative. There should be minimal pictures or animation or videos, but if there are, they should be adequately described and tagged.

- **Page Depth.** Your Funnel should be no more than three clicks away from the main page of your website. That is to say you should be no deeper than three levels from the beginning page.

Campaign Channels, Platforms, and Target communities

Quite simply, a channel just describes the tools you're going to be using to conduct the campaign. Maybe you'll be emphasizing the use of your blog and social network Community? In another campaign, maybe you'd emphasize the use of podcasts, microblogging, or video? Perhaps in this campaign, you'd want to emphasize the use of your blog?

Thereafter, match the appropriate storyteller to the right channel and to assign them that role. It will be that storyteller's responsibility to write content for the blog; to produce video for YouTube; to prepare presentations; to update followers on twitter; to build community on Facebook or Linked-In.

Strategic Outcomes

What you expect to happen with your social media campaign? What's the overall benefit? There's an easy way to be able to think about this by using a spreadsheet or a table.

As a header for the first column, write in *Goal*; for the second column, write in *Funnel*; for the third, write in *Conversion*; the fourth, *Metric*; the fifth, *Current Value*; and the sixth, *Desired Change*.

What you'll end up with is clarity on the specific outcomes you're anticipating by engaging the campaign, and it describes how this campaign will affect your overall Business Goals. Here are just a few examples of how you could use the system.

- Goal: Increase Sales Leads

- Funnel: Your Destination's Contact Us Request Form

- Conversion: Completed Form

- Metric: Number of Requests

- Current Value: 0

- Desired Change: +5%

- Goal: Increase Brand Awareness

- Funnel: Your Destination's Newsletter Page

- Conversion: e-Newsletter Subscriptions

- Metric: Number of Subscriptions

- Current Value: 100

- Desired Change: 20% (20 new subscriptions)

- Goal: Increase Social Networking Engagement

- Funnel: Your Company's Facebook Page

- Conversion: Likes

- Metric: Number of Likes

- Current Value: 2/week

- Desired Change: 4/week

- Goal: Increased Phone Calls

- Funnel: Your Destination's Contact Us Page

- Conversion: A Telephone Call

- Metric: Number of Calls

- Current Value: 7/week

- Desired Change: 10/week

- Goal: More Influence

- Funnel: Your Company's Twitter Account

- Conversion: Follower

- Metric: Number of Followers

- Current Value: 500

- Desired Change: 10% (50 new followers)

- Goal: Increased Online Sales for Product-X

- Funnel: Website eCatalog

- Conversion: Committed Sale

- Metric: Number of Sales

- Current Value: 20 units/month

- Desired Change: +5%/month

Remember that the point in measuring is about accountability. Your storytellers are accountable to help meet these goals and to be able to carry out the strategy as outlined; your social media manager is responsible for meaningful objectives.

Be specific in creating these outcomes and limit to just one or two possibilities; again, one social media campaign can't do everything. The accountability issues important, especially to those who may be watching the success of social media as a marketing strategy. Politically, it's important to establish a meaningful objective and to be able to demonstrate – in practical and measurable ways – that the social media strategy met those objectives. Without accountability, it's very unlikely that social media campaigns could continue because they'd otherwise be based purely on blind faith. *It must be working – I know it, I can feel it!* Most business owners I know aren't that *faithful* to *assumption*.

Measuring ROI

Finally, how will you measure the overall effectiveness of this campaign? All campaigns must have some kind of determination of effectiveness. Will it be a Traditional Metric that attempts to be able to demonstrate return on investment, or, first-order improvements that suggest a Return on Influence? What are the potential affects and how will those metrics be calculated or examined?

Okay, Now You're Ready to Run!

Now that the campaign plan is written up, drafted, circulated, and approved, you're ready execute! Now it's time to carry it off! Cycle through one campaign for 15 days and at the end of the 15 days, complete another plan and run with that.

Maintain copies of your plan. You'll eventually use them as political instruments to demonstrate campaign effectiveness. Over time, your successes and your failures will be documented by the campaign plan, and they can be evaluated by any interested party. They'll see how you planned, organized, executed a strong social media campaign. You will be able to articulate what kinds of returns that were achieved what kind of Influence was purchased by running the campaign. Through examination of second-order effects, you'll be able to demonstrate how the campaign contributed to the bottom line of your organization. You'll even be able to defend your methods to even the most scrutinizing of managerial inquisition! In short, you will develop a working history of successfully managing a social media campaign that promotes your products and services that meaningfully contributed to the success of your company.

Now who wouldn't want that?

Follow-up Questions

1. Think about your current social media efforts. Who's in charge? How is their performance measured and their successes promoted and praised within your organization?

2. Is there executive oversight and commitment to social media? Or is it simply another fad?

3. How is social media being used to make real-world changes in your organization? How is your listening strategy transforming your company? How're you learning from your customers?

4. How can a structured social media campaign plan provide measurable value to your company?

5. Are the Beginning Elements described in Part Five currently in existence for your company? If not, what would it take to get started on the basics?

6. Is your company currently using Pull, Promotion, or Community Strategies? How effective have they been? Do you have the right storytellers?

7. Are there political problems in convincing staff of the importance of social media? How can a structured social media campaign address their political concerns? How can metrics from the campaign demonstrate positive value?

8. What are your competitors doing with social media that you're not?

9. What are the three most important Business Goals for you? How could you use social media in the next year to address them?

10. How can social media change your business' culture for the better?

References

TTYL

I started social networking when I was eleven except it was a little different back then. It was done on computers that'd barely pass as calculators today that'd talk to each computer at ridiculously slow communication speeds. This was the era of the Bulletin Board System (BBS).

BBS' were owned and operated by computer enthusiasts who spent what time and resources they had to create a community where like-minded geeks could dial-up, login one at a time, and leave a message to each other. The computers were in their living rooms or garages. There were no pretty graphics, no video, no pleasantries whatsoever: just text scrolling across a black and white or barely-color monitor. It was slow and tedious. But it was the beginning.

It was the start of how people were changing the use of a computer from a productivity product to a communications product. At the age of eleven, I had friends all over the world that I'd never met or even talked to on a telephone, and one-by-one, we'd all login to a separate bulletin board and post messages to one another and talk about everything – from science, to physics, to comic books, to philosophy, to computer stuff. It was very nerdy. Before I was eighteen, I was running my own BBS and interconnected it to a network of thousands of other systems called FidoNET. It was a golden age for me and it was a time where hardly anybody today would even recognize the tech we used as being "social". Yet that's where I learned the value of community and how to build electronic spaces where people could learn, live, and interact.

Luckily, the times and technology – particularly the connection speeds – have changed. The concepts, though, remain fundamentally the same except today we all use computers to extend our lives, to connect with others everywhere, to overcome isolation, loneliness, and boredom, to share, and to experience a sense of community much larger than ourselves. Not just geeks.

I hope that you found this material useful. I hope you'll continue researching this topic and build a social media campaign strategy for your business, and that you're able to leverage social media to truly astound your customers. It's been my objective in this book to shape ideas rather than instruct on how to use the technology for getting caught up in the latest and greatest social gadget and software really isn't the point. Rather, for business, it's about competitive advantage, and I believe social media has a great deal to offer an enterprising small business who desires to get closer to their customers within electronic spaces where people learn, live, and interact, share, and create a community larger than itself. So get out there and apply this stuff.

We had a saying back in the BBS days that'd we use to sign-off of our messages. TTYL – Talk To You Later – was a common sign-off message that suggested we'd have a chance to meet again online and chit-chat later. It wasn't so much a 'farewell' as a reminder that we'd be talking again and seeing each other again soon … online.

I'd really love to hear your opinions on this work to help improve future revisions. Your feedback and time – your connection – are extremely valuable. I hope we can stay in-touch. Thanks for reading.

TTYL

www.ingramcontent.com/pod-product-compliance
Lightning Source LLC
Chambersburg PA
CBHW071208050326
40689CB00011B/2278